Praise for *The Communication Clinic*

"This book is a prescription for professional success! It provides the treatment needed to best present yourself in writing, speaking, and everyday communication. A must-have reference tool in every professional's cabinet."

—Paula M. Agosto RN, MHA, Chief Nurse Officer,
The Children's Hospital of Philadelphia

"In this age of 24-hour tweets and social media outreach, *The Communication Clinic* is a thoughtful and accessible guide for anyone—from student to professional—on how to enhance important communication skills. I expect that this well-designed book will become a 'must-have' for any teacher, human resources professional, or corporate officer that advises on career strategies. But most of all, it should be a must for every job seeker who wants to stand out in today's competitive market place."

—Arlene Morgan, Assistant Dean,
External Affairs, Temple University School of Media
and Communication; formerly Associate Dean,
Columbia Journalism School

"Simply put, communication skills are the key to workplace success. And Pachter and Cowie show you how, simply and effectively. The authors bring a lifetime of experience sharpening prose, and lay out the techniques good writers and speakers use in plain, straightforward English. If you want to write more clearly, give better presentations, and most of all, be listened to, the rules and tips in this book are essential."

—Andy Cassel, formerly Editor in Chief at
Moody's Analytics; former *Philadelphia Inquirer*
columnist, "The Economy"

"Pachter and Cowie have authored yet another great resource for business professionals! Many of the tips included in this book are essential to achieving success and/or avoiding mistakes that can impact one's career."

—Jim Alexander, PharmD, Executive Director and
Founder, Industry Pharmacists Organization

"All readers, those just beginning their careers as well as seasoned professionals, will benefit from the insightful advice provided by Barbara and Denise across a wide range of real life business situations. Covering topics as simple as everyday email etiquette to far more complex situations where discretion and judgment are necessary, the guidance provided in this book will help ensure successful results from all communications."

—Cathy Pulos, Senior Vice President,
Chief People Officer and CFO, Wawa, Inc.

"Pachter and Cowie have done an excellent job of providing more useful information for professionals at all stages of their careers. By using real-life dilemmas from the business environment, they provide extremely helpful and practical solutions to those issues and misadventures that can derail careers. Their prescriptions for success will provide much-needed lifelines to those who are floundering and bolster those who are already fans of their message."

—Joseph A. Barone, PharmD, FCCP,
Dean and Professor,
Ernest Mario School of Pharmacy

THE
COMMUNICATION
CLINIC

99 PROVEN CURES FOR THE MOST COMMON BUSINESS MISTAKES

BARBARA PACHTER
AND DENISE COWIE

New York Chicago San Francisco Athens London
Madrid Mexico City Milan New Delhi
Singapore Sydney Toronto

1 2 3 4 5 6 7 8 9   LCR   21 20 19 18 17 16

ISBN   978-1-259-64484-9
MHID   1-259-64484-7

e-ISBN   978-1-259-64485-6
e-MHID   1-259-64485-5

This publication is designed to provide accurate and authoritative information in regard to the subject matter covered. It is sold with the understanding that neither the author nor the publisher is engaged in rendering legal, accounting, securities trading, or other professional services. If legal advice or other expert assistance is required, the services of a competent professional person should be sought.

—*From a Declaration of Principles Jointly Adopted*
by a Committee of the American Bar Association
and a Committee of Publishers and Associations

McGraw-Hill Education books are available at special quantity discounts to use as premiums and sales promotions or for use in corporate training programs. To contact a representative, please visit the Contact Us pages at www.mhprofessional.com.

This book is dedicated to our husbands,
Martin Heiligman and L. Stuart Ditzen,
who were (almost) always patient and supportive,
even when their wives became increasingly
preoccupied as deadlines loomed.

Contents

PART I | BUSINESS WRITING IN A DIGITAL WORLD

PART II | PRESENTATION SKILLS: TALK YOUR WAY TO THE TOP

PART III | TALK ISN'T CHEAP: ASSERTIVE COMMUNICATION AND CONFLICT

PART IV | IT'S YOUR RESPONSIBILITY:
CAREER ADVANCEMENT AND JOB SEARCH

PART V | THE FINISHING TOUCHES: YOUR ACTIONS AND APPEARANCE MAKE A DIFFERENCE

Acknowledgments

This book was written with the input of many people—participants in seminars who shared their experiences, executives who came to Barbara for coaching, reporters who needed up-to-date information, and the many "strangers" who wrote asking for help. Their stories, experiences, and questions made us think, rethink, and fine-tune how to communicate effectively in today's business world.

We would like to thank Casie Vogel, our former editor, who introduced us to Leila Campoli, our agent. Leila tirelessly pushed for this book to be written and introduced us to our current editor, Cheryl Ringer. Cheryl, a rising star at McGraw-Hill Professional, kept us on our toes and made us better communicators. Never underestimate the power of networking! A special thank-you to Joyce Hoff, who acted as referee and sounding board. And a tip of the hat to each other, for many years of working together successfully.

—*Barbara and Denise*

Introduction

The Communication Clinic is an invaluable guidebook for business people at all levels in the workplace. Not only will it help you to diagnose your areas of concern in business communication, but it will provide you with a prescription for future success.

How you communicate with others—whether in person, in writing, or online—has a tremendous impact on your career. It affects every aspect of your working life, no matter how good your specialized skills are in your particular field.

Consider this email sent to Barbara Pachter's office:

> *Greetings! I'm doing social media work and my boss has taken my project from me bc of some typos on my post. I don't feel this is right... What is the best way to handle this situation and get my project back? I would any advice you may have...I have only been a professional for 3years and I don't always knw HOW to handle situations like this.*

This entry-level professional is not alone in experiencing the consequences of poor communication, nor in failing to recognize how to deal with the problem.

Consider the many professionals who know how to perform their jobs but find their prospects for advancement diminished because their lack of social skills affects their ability to develop relationships. Think of the legions who fail to express their ideas clearly, whether they are writing an email or making a presentation, so their voices go unheeded and their potential contributions are ignored. And then there are those who don't realize how their words come across to others and may inadvertently create conflicts that harm their careers—and sometimes their companies.

Yet many of these individuals—regardless of how many years they have been in the business world—are left wondering why they haven't advanced in their careers. You don't want your communication shortcomings to derail your career before you have a chance to find out what you might have accomplished.

The Communication Clinic will allow you to recognize the mistakes that may be holding you back, and help you to overcome them. It will equip you with the tools to avoid potential career stumbling blocks, and it will encourage you to become a confident and effective communicator.

The guidelines of this book are grounded firmly in the real world of business, based on the authors' years of interaction with workers at all levels and in numerous fields—from manufacturing and healthcare to technology and finance. However, where examples are used, all names, job titles, company names, or any other identifying information has been changed.

The step-by-step instructions, prescriptions for success, and occasional exercises are helpful for anyone seeking to improve communication skills and professionalism.

Topics covered include:

- Writing an effective email
- Crafting a blog post
- Developing a professional presence
- Mastering verbal and nonverbal communication
- Using social media for career success
- Making a successful presentation
- Dining for business
- Being assertive (not aggressive) in person and online
- Managing conflict
- Conducting an effective job search

Barbara Pachter has taught communication to tens of thousands of participants in corporate seminars and university classes for many years. She has coached hundreds of professionals on how to present themselves in the workplace and advance in their careers. Denise Cowie has spent her career writing and editing for newspapers, and more recently for magazines and websites. She understands how important it is to communicate clearly.

Though this book contains the work of both authors, it is Barbara Pachter's voice that appears on these pages.

The Communication Clinic is not a book to read in one sitting. We encourage you to work on a few entries at a time, putting the suggestions into practice and doing the exercises that enforce what you learn. For this reason, we have tried to make each segment as comprehensive as possible, cross-referencing to additional relevant information where necessary.

We anticipate that you—and others—will gradually notice an improvement in your communication skills. We are confident that the effort you make now will pay off handsomely in the future, enriching your career.

PART I

BUSINESS WRITING IN A DIGITAL WORLD

We live and work in an age where technology is constantly changing the way we communicate. One thing, however, hasn't changed, and that is the importance of our words and the need to write them effectively, regardless of whether we are writing an email, sending a text, posting on social media, or even writing a letter.

Words have power, and written words have lasting power.

When you connect in writing to coworkers, bosses, vendors, customers, colleagues, potential employers, or clients, you reveal a great deal about yourself, and often the company for which you work. And even though the business world is more informal today than in the past, it doesn't mean that you can be sloppy or rude.

Do you think the following written comments send the message that the writers carefully considered their words? Would you make assumptions about the people who wrote these sentences?

hey tom, i need to remember that!!!!

Working in Customer Service we deal with customers on daily bases.

YOU GUYS HAVE FAILED TO PROVIDE THE NECESSARY DOCUMENTATION . . .

To get the information I sent an email to a worker at a different department who I was informed was knowledgeable in a subject I had a question about.

A poorly written email or post on social media can have disastrous effects on your business relationships, and ultimately on your career.

Over the last 20 years, I have collected thousands of writing samples from the participants in my corporate seminars and students in my university classes. I also have received hundreds of emails and texts from the readers of my books, people who have seen my blog, and others who have read articles quoting me in the media. Samples from many of these sources are used during my seminars, and also in this section, but names, job titles, company names, and locations have been altered. Anything that might reveal who wrote an example has been changed.

Follow the suggestions in this section and learn from the examples of others so that your written words convey that you are a professional and an effective communicator.

1. "I Didn't Know That!"
The Essentials of Good Business Writing

A sales manager was going on vacation and emailed his customers, giving them the name of a person to contact in his absence. Unfortunately, he gave the wrong email address for that person. He lost some sales as a result.

A colleague forces me to work to understand what he writes when he goes on and on in his emails. Sometimes I get it right. Other times, I don't! I would never want to work with him on a full-time basis.

Your job, your work relationships, or your business can suffer if you don't write effectively, as these two comments illustrate. This is true regardless of your position, your industry, or your age and experience.

It's important to write professionally, but that can be difficult to do if you were never taught the essentials of business writing, nor realized the consequences of poor writing.

Your writing can improve significantly when you understand the importance of these five essentials. Good business writing needs to be:

1. **Clear.** Your readers need to understand what you have written the first time they read your comments. People don't want to have to reread a sentence two or three times to make sure they have read it correctly. If your message is difficult to grasp—whether because of the wording, layout of the email, or amount of detail—your readers will agree with famed American novelist Kurt Vonnegut, who said, "If you can't write clearly, you probably don't think nearly as well as you think you do."

2. **Concise.** You waste people's time when you include unnecessary words. Write what you need to say in as few words as necessary.

3. **Error free.** Anyone can make an error occasionally. But if you consistently make mistakes, or have a number of them in any one document, your reputation will suffer and miscommunication can occur.

4. **Conversational.** If you write in a conversational manner, you are more apt to connect with your reader. Use words that your reader readily understands. Why use a phrase such as "Pursuant to our discussion . . ." if you don't use it when speaking with someone? Wouldn't using "As we discussed . . ." be easier for your reader to grasp?

5. **Understood by your reader.** If you do the first four items, this fifth essential is more likely to occur: Your overall meaning will be understood by your reader. That is your ultimate goal, because if you write to people and they don't understand what you are trying to communicate, have you accomplished anything?

Now that you know what good business writing requires, it's time to get to work on the details. The suggestions in this section will help you make the five essentials part of your writing routine and make your communications more professional.

PRESCRIPTION FOR SUCCESS

Remember that email can easily be forwarded to others, which means that email can be the "gift" that keeps on giving. Your poorly written email may be seen by many others — even if you didn't intend for that to happen.

2. Getting Started: Five Ways to Overcome Writer's Block

Every time I sit down at the computer I realize I have no idea what I'm doing and my girlfriend has to listen to me whine about how lost and confused and untalented I am. But hopefully, if you do something often enough you get in the habit and pretty soon instinct takes over.

After I saw the play *Clybourne Park*, I read the above quote by the playwright, Bruce Norris, and knew that I had to show it to the participants in my corporate writing classes. Many of them believe that they are the only ones who have difficulty getting started with their writings. Even someone like Norris, who won the 2011 Pulitzer Prize for drama for this play, has trouble figuring out the right words.

Writer's block can affect all types of writers, including businesspeople. Consider these comments from some of the participants in my classes:

I sit down to write and nothing comes. It's frustrating!

I put off my writing assignments as long as I can.

I find other people to do my writing assignments.

There are numerous ways to overcome writer's block. Try some of the following:

1. **Take a short break.** The emphasis here is on "short." A change of scenery can clear your head so that when you get back to work you are more refreshed and open to writing. Take a short walk, talk to a colleague, or do some stretches. Some writers say they like to iron, others do the dishes—but these activities are hard for most of us to do at work!

2. **Schedule time to write.** Some people think that the only cure for writer's block is to write. And if you schedule the time on your calendar, you are more likely to keep to your plan and write. I know that in some jobs, setting aside a dedicated block of time to write can be difficult, but if you think about your day, you often can arrange some writing time.

3. **Control your interruptions.** You need an uninterrupted period of time to write. It does you no good to set aside some time for writing if you are going to be distracted time after time by people visiting or by your own compulsion to keep checking email. One woman had to write a monthly report, but it took her a day and a half to write it in the office because she had so many interruptions. Finally, she got permission to work from home one morning each month and found she could write the report in three hours. That's a big difference! Also avoid roaming around the Internet. An unknown source said, "Being a good writer is 3 percent talent, 97 percent not being distracted by the Internet."

4. **Set a deadline.** Most people, if they have a deadline, will work hard to meet it. Reporters generally don't have the luxury of suffering from writer's block because they have deadlines. Set one for yourself, or have your supervisor set one for you. And when you meet your deadline, go ahead and reward yourself. I have always found chocolate chip cookies a great reward!

5. **Cluster your topic.** Clustering, also called mind mapping, can help you identify what you know about your topic, which makes getting started easier. Put the subject of your writing assignment—whether it's a sales presentation, a performance appraisal, or an evaluation of new software—in the center of a sheet of paper, and then jot down any thoughts that come to mind about your topic. Do not write full sentences, just key words. Even if your thoughts seem silly, include them anyway. Place related subjects together (see illustration). Once you have jotted down all the ideas you can think of, cross out the ones you don't need, and number the rest in the order you will write about them. You will now be ready to start writing.

Clustering or Mind Mapping

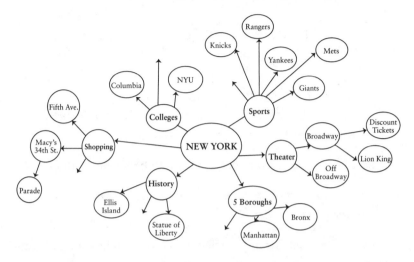

The next chapter, "Imperfect Writing for Perfect Results," outlines the steps you should take from here.

PRESCRIPTION FOR SUCCESS

Don't limit the use of clustering to your own writings. It's a great way to harness collective brainpower if your team is working on a project, or if you are looking for patterns to common problems. You know those "murder boards" that are so beloved by the detectives on television shows? They're just another form of clustering!

3. Imperfect Writing for Perfect Results

I write a couple of sentences and then delete them. Write a few more and delete them. It's a constant, incredibly annoying process.

I always have to rewrite. Is there something wrong with me?

I was afraid to apply for a new position because it involved a lot of writing.

The above comments from participants in my writing seminars illustrate the frustration businesspeople often feel when tackling writing assignments. But it's not just participants in such classes who suffer from fear of writing. Putting pen to paper—or fingers to keyboard—can be daunting for many people.

I believe that, to a large degree, the frustration comes from people trying to create a perfect piece of writing the first time they sit down to do an assignment, whether it's a business email or a complicated report. They mistakenly think that what they type should not need any correcting or rewriting. But creating an imperfect piece of writing—a draft—is part of the normal process of writing. Yes, I said normal.

Once you have a draft, you can set about revising it. Most people find it easier to correct their writing than to create the exact wording they want the first time they try. Many well-known people, including professional writers, have expressed their understanding of the importance of writing . . . and rewriting.

There is no great writing, only great rewriting. —Louis Brandeis, Supreme Court justice

The first draft is a skeleton . . . just bare bones. The rest of the story comes later with revising. —Judy Blume, author

I'm not a very good writer, but I'm an excellent rewriter.
—*James Michener, author*

I describe the making of the draft as "open writing." This term is easy to remember, as you basically open yourself up and let the words flow. Here are five guidelines to help you with open writing:

1. **Relax.** People have a tendency to get nervous and then agonize over their writing assignments. Remember, it doesn't have to be perfect yet. One seminar participant told me that once the pressure was off to create a perfect draft on her first attempt, she was able to write.

2. **Write the way you speak.** Most of us have no difficulty speaking coherently and clearly. When you write the way you speak, you are writing in a conversational tone, which helps you connect with your reader. Another advantage is that this approach often helps you write quickly.

3. **Don't stop writing.** No crossing out or backspacing. You don't want to disrupt the flow of your thoughts. If you find yourself going off in the wrong direction, write yourself out of it. You will rearrange your wording later. Computers make it very easy to cut and paste text. (This term survives from a time when writers revising on paper literally had to cut up their written phrases and paste them in the order they preferred. We have it so much easier now!)

4. **Set a time limit.** When you sit down to write, allocate a certain amount of time to the task. It doesn't need to be a lot of time. In my classes, my writing assignments are only five minutes in duration, but all the participants write between half a page and a page and a half. That's a lot of writing in just a few minutes. After my students have finished their open writing assignments, I tell them that in the past, most of them have stared at a blank computer screen for longer than five minutes. Now consider how much they've been able to write in the same time in class. That is when the lightbulb goes on for them, and they realize the value of open writing.

5. **Don't worry about spelling or grammar . . . for now.** You will correct your grammar and spelling before you hit the send button or mail that document. For now, you just want to write.

Once you have followed these five steps, keep in mind that you are *not* done. Let me say that again: You are not done. Now it is time to revise your writing—a task that's addressed in the following chapters—but now you have something to work on, instead of a blank screen.

PRESCRIPTION FOR SUCCESS

Opening sentences are important, but don't let crafting "the perfect one" stop you from getting started. Just jot down whatever comes into your head and continue with the rest of the draft. Once you have written a fair amount, go back and review your opening. You'll find you have a much clearer idea of what your opening should say.

4. Looks Count: Make Your Writings Visually Appealing

A woman in one of my writing seminars said she sent a meeting announcement to her teammates and used 30-point red type in a bold font to get their attention. She did get their attention—but not in a good way. Her teammates didn't like that her chosen techniques for emphasis—large type, use of a bright color, exclamation points, and bold font style—made her appear to be screaming at them. As a result, her boss sent her to my class!

Many people don't think about the visual appearance of their documents and the impact that has on the reader and the readability of the email.

The placement of the words on a page (or screen), the use of emphasis techniques, and the choice of font, type size, and color often determine whether your documents are read. You don't want your emails to shout at or overwhelm your reader or be difficult to read.

The following suggestions should help you to increase the readability of your emails:

1. **Avoid paragraphs that are too long.** When paragraphs are very long, they become what I call a sheet of black ice, causing readers' eyes to slide right over the text. My general guideline is that you want your paragraphs to be no longer than nine lines. But that doesn't mean every paragraph should be nine lines. The key to increasing readability is to *vary the length* of your paragraphs. You can have paragraphs longer than nine lines and as short as one line. This difference in paragraph lengths adds vitality to your writings. (Look at the varied lengths of the paragraphs above.)

2. **Include a blank line between paragraphs.** Your paragraphs can merge into one large block of type if you don't add white space between them.

3. **Use an appropriate font size, type, and color.** Using either very large or very small type sizes, fancy fonts, or several different colors can make it difficult for people to read your message quickly. Generally, it is best to use 10- or 12-point type and an easy-to-read font, such as Arial, Calibri, Times New Roman, Verdana, or Georgia. Handwriting fonts, such as Lucida Handwriting, are very difficult to read when used as body text. Black and dark blue are the best colors for email type.

4. **Avoid writing text in all capital letters.** Using all capital letters is the written equivalent of shouting. What's more, it is difficult to read. Don't use all lowercase letters, either—that, too, is hard to read. All caps may be used for headings or the occasional word for emphasis.

5. **Avoid long sentences.** They are more difficult to read and understand. Studies of business writing suggest that sentences should average about 15 to 17 words in length. But that doesn't mean every sentence should be 16 words. The key to increasing the readability of sentences, just like paragraphs, is to *vary their length*. This means using some short, some medium, and some long sentences. As you probably know from your own experience, it's difficult to grasp the meaning of a sentence that is too wordy. How many times would you have to read the following sentence to understand its message?

> *To assist us in the development of the annual budget and to permit the inclusion therein of "one time" major expenditure items required for the operation of your department, you are requested to submit your anticipated requirements in order of descending priority for the calendar year. (46 words)*

6. **Use headings to divide your documents into sections.** This makes it easy for readers to see quickly what areas you will be discussing. *The Gregg Reference Manual*, a well-respected style guide, has several pages illustrating different headings. Yet using headings doesn't have to be complicated. For most business emails, your headings can be either in bold type or in all caps.

Bullets, too, can be used to set off sections of a document. The next chapter looks in greater detail at the ways in which bullet points and bulleted lists can make your writings more appealing and easier to read.

QUESTION TO CONSIDER

Q. *A colleague told me I was overdoing my use of exclamation marks. I often use three or four at the end of my sentences to make a point. Am I wrong?*

A. Not if you are writing a comic book! In business writing, exclamation marks can be used occasionally to convey excitement and enthusiasm, but use them sparingly. If you use more than one at the end of a sentence, or too many in any one email, it is overwhelming. Don't do it.

PRESCRIPTION FOR SUCCESS

Avoid using red pencil or pen to make corrections for yourself or others. It can bring back bad memories from school, when teachers used red pencils to correct our writings. As one of my corporate participants recalled:

> I once had a manager who had the (bad) habit of using a red pen on my emails. He would print them out and return them to me with red "notes" all over the place. Although I learned a great deal about my writing, I suffered greatly every time I had to copy him on any email I wrote.

5. These Bullets Won't Kill Your Writing

When I started highlighting important points in my emails with bullets, I got better responses. I should have started using them sooner.

I got my emails down to one screen when I starting using lists. I thought my clients would want me to write more. No one ever asked for more!

Many professionals I have coached have made comments about bullets that are similar to those above. With good reason. Using a bulleted list improves the visual appearance of your document and makes it easier for the reader to grasp your concepts. Your key items stand out.

Bulleted lists also require less writing, and as a result, many people make fewer mistakes. In addition, email recipients can copy the list, paste it into their replies, and respond to each bullet point individually.

As the previous chapter explained, there are numerous ways to improve the layout of your documents. Using a bulleted list is an additional one. But don't shoot yourself in the foot. Use these general guidelines to add bullets successfully:

- **Start the list with an *opening statement* that ends with a colon.** For example:

  My current position involves a series of tasks, including:
  - Answering customer calls
  - Providing information about our products
  - Referring callers to additional sites for more information
  - Logging calls for future reference

- **Make sure your bullet items have parallel structure.** Each line should start with the same form. This is frequently a noun or a verb—often ending in the *-ing* form, as in the example above. Capitalize the first word after the bullet.

- **Be consistent with your bullet style.** Word processing gives you a number of choices, including circles, squares, triangles, and even circles within circles. Don't become overly creative. Pick one style of bullet, and use that throughout your document.

- **Use numbers, not bullets, if there is a sequence of steps to follow.** This helps to avoid confusion. When you use numbers for such a sequence, people naturally assume number 1 is the first step. But if you use numbers instead of bullets when the points are not sequential, people may assume number 1 is the most important—which may or may not be the case.

- **Have at least two, but no more than eight, bullets in a list.** If you use too many bullets in any one list, it will be distracting. Too many bulleted lists in any one document will be distracting to the reader also.

- **If the bullet points are sentences, the ending punctuation mark is a period.** If the points are questions, end with a question mark. No closing punctuation is needed if the bullet point is a single word or phrase.

- **Use bold type.** You can emphasize the first sentence in a bullet point by putting it in boldface type (as we have done for this bulleted list).

PRESCRIPTION FOR SUCCESS

Review your writings. Have you been using lists? If not, would adding lists have made it easier for your reader to grasp your concepts? If you have been using bullet points, have you followed the guidelines in this chapter?

6. Simple Words *Are Not* for Simple People

I wanted to impress my colleagues with my large vocabulary.

I want my boss to think I'm smart, so I use big words.

My response to comments such as these from participants in my seminars is to quote Albert Einstein, a pretty smart guy, who said, "If you can't explain it simply, you don't know it well enough."

Einstein didn't feel a need to prove how intellectually superior he was—and you shouldn't, either.

You don't impress people by using long, unfamiliar words. You impress them when you write clearly and concisely—using commonly known words that enable your readers to understand your comments quickly.

I love this sentence from Steve Jobs's Stanford commencement speech in 2005, a talk that has been viewed more than 8 million times on YouTube:

And most important, have the courage to follow your heart and intuition.

Would it have had the same appeal if he had said the following?

And most important, have the courage to follow your heart and intuitive cognition.

Not likely!

I would have had to look up *intuitive cognition*—which brings up one of three good reasons to avoid using "big words" unnecessarily:

1. **People don't like to look up words.** It takes time to look up the meaning of a word—even with built-in dictionaries on computers and iPads. It may be only a little hassle, but people still don't want to do it. Can you recall the last time you looked up a word

you didn't know? Many don't bother and simply skip over the word—which doesn't help you if you want your readers to understand your comments.

2. **People have to figure out what you are trying to say.** A couple of years ago, this sentence was in an email from a colleague: "Reflecting on the winter, I am resolved not to think disparagingly over any of our inflated summer temperatures." I believe she was trying to impress me, but I was not impressed, as it took me a while to figure out what the sentence meant.

3. **You may use the word incorrectly.** The less familiar you are with a word, the more likely you are to use it incorrectly, or not quite correctly. The sentence "I'm a motivated self-starter with amplitude for discovery" was in one seminar participant's email to me. I assume he was trying to say he had a great *aptitude* for discovery. *Amplitude* can describe an abundance of something—an amplitude of emotion, for example—but it is probably most often used to describe specific actions in mathematics or physics.

Using simpler words doesn't mean that your writings will be dull or that you are talking down to people. Our language is full of lively, descriptive words that are in common use. You can write interestingly, persuasively, and clearly without searching out 10-dollar words that may only muddy your meaning.

The bottom line (or *resolution* or *solution*, if you wish) is to use words that *your reader* understands. Remember what master wordsmith Mark Twain said, in the days when writers were paid by the word: "I never write *metropolis* for seven cents because I can get the same price for *city*. I never write *policeman* because I can get the same money for *cop*."

Exercise

Review the following list. Do you have a tendency to write with words like those on the left? Would it be easier for your readers if you used words like those on the right? When you edit your writings, try substituting words on the right for those on the left, and consider whether your statements are now more easily understood.

Ameliorate	improve/make better
Capricious	fickle/inconsistent
Endeavor	try
Eradicate	eliminate/get rid of
Extricate	remove from/free from
Peruse	read
Solicit	ask
Utilize	use

QUESTION TO CONSIDER

Q. *There are certain technical words that are unique to my profession. Can I use those?*

A. Yes, you can. Just make sure that everyone who is receiving the email will be able to understand what those terms mean. Take into consideration the following excellent writing objective, which was given to me by a corporate client:

> Present technical information in a clear and concise manner so that nontechnical people understand the basic concepts presented.

PRESCRIPTION FOR SUCCESS

Use a thesaurus. If you are unsure whether you should use a particular word, consult the thesaurus for different choices and pick the one that is appropriate for your reader.

7. Do Not Use Contractions
(Don't Worry, I Didn't Mean It!)

During a recent conversation with a colleague, I mentioned that my next blog was going to be on contractions. "Contractions?" she all but shouted. "Nobody should use contractions!" Then she explained that when she was growing up, her teachers drilled into her head that she should never use contractions in her writing. Her teachers maintained, and she still believed, that contractions are too informal and sloppy.

Many people in my writing seminars tell me similar stories.

A contraction, according to *The Gregg Reference Manual,* is "a shortened form of a word or phrase in which an apostrophe indicates the omitted letters or words: For example, *don't* for *do not.*"

My response to my colleague and to the participants in my seminars is always the same: "Why can't we use contractions? We use them when we speak, so why isn't it okay to write with them?"

A primary goal of writing is to connect with your reader, and your choice of words helps to make that connection. Nonverbal clues cannot help to make your point when you email someone because the reader doesn't see the smile on your face or hear the friendly tone of your voice. (Yes, I know there are emoticons, but I do not encourage their use in business writing.)

Using contractions helps you to convey a conversational tone. It makes the communication sound more personal and friendly and less like a directive. Listen to the difference: "Let's go to the conference on Monday," or "Let us go to the conference on Monday." Don't you think the second version sounds rather stilted?

Here are suggestions for using contractions successfully in business writing:

1. **Think about your use of contractions.** It may not be first on your list of business concerns, but the quality of your writing is important. Do you use contractions? It's fine to do so, judiciously.

2. **Do not overuse them.** Just because you can use contractions in your writing in today's business world doesn't mean you should always use them. Read your documents out loud to hear how your use of contractions sounds. If your writings sound choppy, chances are you are using too many contractions. One of my interns had the courage to point out to me that I used contractions a lot. I hadn't realized just how much until she said something. I really valued that feedback.

3. **Avoid excessively casual contractions.** Some contractions sound sloppy. For example: "You'd" for "you would" or "she's" for "she has." I recommend not using them in business writing. And please, don't ever be tempted by double contractions, such as "shouldn't've" for "should not have."

4. **Know what your boss prefers.** If your boss does not want you to use contractions, don't! This is not (isn't) rocket science, and it is not worth fighting over.

5. **Understand the difference between *it's* and *its*.** A common mistake involves the difference between *it's*—which is the contraction for "it is"—and the possessive *its*. A way to remember the difference between them is that the apostrophe in *it's* means a letter is missing. If you aren't sure, read your sentence aloud and then substitute the noncontraction form (in this case, "it is") to see whether it still makes sense. ("It's time to put the pencil in its case," for example. If you had an erroneous apostrophe in the second *its*, the sentence wouldn't make sense.) People often use the wrong form in their writings, and others love to point out their mistakes. Don't give them the opportunity!

Your use of contractions may not seem like a big deal, but it is one of the many little things that can impact your writings and is therefore worthy of your attention.

PRESCRIPTION FOR SUCCESS

Sometimes contractions are safer. If you are writing a report in which the absence of the word *not* would change the meaning of your message entirely, play it safe and use the contraction, as in "He didn't go ahead with the project" instead of "He did not go ahead with the project." This way, you cannot accidentally leave out the essential *not*, and your readers cannot subconsciously read over it.

8. "But I Didn't Mean It That Way!" How to Eliminate a Harsh Tone in Your Emails

I don't understand why he responded so negatively.

People always tell me I have a nasty tone. I don't get it!

A common concern people have expressed in my writing classes is that they inadvertently appear harsh in their emails. As the above quotes indicate, they don't realize that their word choices and what they include in their emails affect the way people interpret their comments. How often have you heard someone say, "But that's not how I meant it"?

In an email, you don't have the nonverbal communication that many of us rely on to soften harsh wording because recipients don't see your face or hear your voice.

These suggestions will help you to eliminate any unpleasant tone in your writing. Some of these items are discussed in other chapters on different topics, but they bear repeating here as a single checklist. When you consider these points together, you can see how they can help you to avoid a harsh or imperious tone.

1. **Include a salutation.** Though not technically required in an email, a salutation is a positive way to begin. It makes you sound friendlier. A simple "Hi Sally" or "Dear Sally" will start your message on a more pleasant note. Also use a closing comment, such as "Best regards" or "Thanks," to eliminate an abrupt ending.

2. **Use positive, not negative, wording.** Many emails acquire a harsh tone simply based on the writer's choice of words. Pay attention to these three areas:

- **Avoid negative words** such as *failure, wrong, blame, nasty,* or *neglected.* What would you rather read: "The premise of your report is totally wrong," or "The premise of your report needs to be reassessed." The first sentence sounds accusatory. The second statement makes the same point without harshness.

- **Use polite language.** Use *please* and *thank you.* One of these directives may sound severe to your reader: "Please finish these updates by the end of the day." Or "Get these updates finished by the end of the day." Which would you rather receive? Also, make sure you say *thank you* to people who have helped you.

- **Emphasize the positive.** Listen to the difference in these two statements: "We will be able to finish the work by December 15," or "We won't be able to finish the work until December 15." The meaning is the same, but the second statement makes the information sound negative.

3. **Don't use all caps.** Occasionally, I will have someone in my class who doesn't know that writing comments in all capital letters is the equivalent of shouting. It is, and people don't like to be yelled at.

4. **Don't repeat information needlessly.** You may insult your reader. People complain, "Why do I have to read the same information three times? I got it the first time."

5. **Go easy on emphasis techniques.** Using bold or bright-colored type (red, purple, etc.), large fonts, or too many exclamation marks can make you sound aggressive.

6. **Read the email out loud before you hit send.** If what you have written sounds harsh to you, it will sound harsh to your reader. Review the points in this list against the wording in your emails, and change whatever is necessary in your emails to make them sound less severe. Make sure you do this step—it is important to avoid misunderstandings.

Exercise

In your effort to eliminate a negative tone, don't put yourself down. By trying not to be harsh, some people use a lot of self-discounting language, including *just*, *actually*, *perhaps*, *I wonder*, and *I hope*. Check your emails against this list:

If you use:	Try this instead:
I hope this is what you were looking for.	Be direct. Write, "If you need additional information, just let me know."
I was wondering if I can attend the meeting?	Be assertive. Delete "I was wondering . . ." and say, "I would like to attend the meeting."
I'm sorry to be a bother . . .	Ask yourself: Why am I a bother? Delete this phrase from your vocabulary.

PRESCRIPTION FOR SUCCESS

Eliminate any curse words. This is so obvious a point that I shouldn't have to mention it. Unfortunately, my experience has taught me otherwise. You can disagree without being disagreeable.

9. Eliminate ~~Those~~ Extra Words

Many noteworthy people have expressed the importance of eliminating unnecessary words in writing:

> *The most valuable of all talents is that of never using two words when one will do. —Thomas Jefferson*

> *I'm sure that it's harder to write shorter and crisper than it is to write long and dull. —John Roberts, chief justice of the Supreme Court*

> *I have made this letter longer than usual, only because I have not had time to make it shorter. —Blaise Pascal, seventeenth-century French philosopher*

The participants in my seminars agree with these quotes. They tell me that their biggest complaint about other people's writings is their use of too many words. (Unfortunately, the people doing the complaining are also using too many words!)

One reason we use extra words is that our teachers often assigned papers with a specific word count. Many of us added unnecessary words to fulfill the word count, encouraging a bad habit. Other reasons include people being unaware of their writing style or not realizing the importance of concise writing.

If you use unnecessary words to communicate with others, your readers may become bogged down in all the verbiage, and your key points may be lost. Plus, extra words make your emails and other documents longer—and the shorter your writing is, the more likely it is to be read.

We add extra words in numerous ways, including:

1. **Needless words.** This is when you use a number of words to express something when a single word would convey the same

meaning. Why write "At this point in time" when the word *now* means the same thing?

Other examples include:

In the event of	when
Show a preference for	prefer
In the majority of instances	usually
Despite the fact that	although
In close proximity to	near
For the reason that	because
Due to the fact that	because
Each and every one	all
For the purpose of	to

2. **Unnecessary modifiers.** This one can be tricky. Modifiers can be effective when they add meaning, as in "Tom volunteered to carry the *heavy* package." *Heavy* is an adjective describing something specific about the package, and this may be important information for your reader. Often, however, modifiers don't add any useful information, as in "He read the *entire* report." *Entire* is not needed. "He read the *entire* report" and "He read the report" mean the same thing.

   Other unnecessary modifiers include such adverbs as *actually*, *really*, and *definitely*, as in "She is *actually* the newest member of the team." *Actually* adds nothing to the sentence but length.

3. **Redundant expressions.** This is when you use several words to express something, but one of those words explicitly means what you are trying to say. This redundancy—using phrases like "assembled together," for example—can give the impression that you don't understand the meaning of your words. *Assembled* means "brought together"; you don't need to include *together*.

   Other examples include:

Brief in duration	brief
Empty out	empty
Fall down	fall

Fewer in number	fewer
File away	file
Heat up	heat
New innovation	innovation
Open up	open
Postponed until later	postponed
Repeat again	repeat

4. **Unnecessary detail.** Don't add supposedly clarifying information that isn't needed. Consider this sentence:

> *The paper that I just read explains the new items in the budget—the items that weren't included last year.*

The phrase "the items that weren't included last year" is already explained by "new items." It is not necessary to describe what "new" means.

Exercise

Rewrite these sentences, eliminating extra words.

1. The completion of the project has been delayed somewhat due to the fact that the vice president changed his mind about hiring additional new personnel.

2. It was an unexpected surprise when the CEO spoke at our conference.

3. As a general rule the manager will send packages scheduled for overnight delivery.

Edited versions are on page 28.

Answers

Here are the corrected sentences for the Exercise on page 27.

1. The project has been delayed because the vice president changed his mind about hiring additional personnel.

2. It was a surprise when the CEO spoke at our conference.

3. Generally, the manager sends packages overnight.

PRESCRIPTION FOR SUCCESS

Edit your writings. Over the next few weeks, review your emails with the pointers given in this chapter in mind. Are you using extra words? If you look for them, you will usually find some. Eliminate them, and see how much crisper and clearer your emails are.

10. Email Rules: Don't Drive Your Readers to Distraction!

It drives me crazy when I email information to people—information that they requested—and they don't acknowledge that they received the email, let alone thank me!

Have you ever felt a similar sentiment? Many have.

I believe strongly that people in the workplace should let you know they have received information you have sent them, and if they requested that information, good manners require that they thank you.

One of my students followed my advice and sent an email to her professor, thanking him for his email answering several of her questions about an upcoming project. The professor was so pleased that the student had thanked him that he gave her two additional points on her project. No student had ever thanked him before!

It is rude when people don't acknowledge your time or effort to help them. Replying with a simple "Thanks" is all that is needed. You can, of course, write more, such as: "Thank you for the information. It will be helpful."

Here are some additional suggestions so you don't drive others crazy with your emails:

1. **Remember that you are writing an email, not a text.** Do not use text shortcuts. All too often, people forget and write "u" for "you" and "GR8" instead of "great," and so on. Email is informal communication, but not that informal. Also avoid text acronyms, such as BAU for "business as usual," as in "I had a slow morning, but this afternoon it was BAU." It is also rare for emoticons or emoji to be appropriate for business email. (Yes, I do know that the "Face with Tears of Joy" emoji was chosen as the 2015 word of the year by the Oxford Dictionaries, and I still don't encourage its use in business.)

2. **Pay attention.** You need to concentrate. If you don't, you can easily send an email before you have finished editing your comments, or send the email to the wrong people. One senior manager wrote to me: "Feel free to use me as an example of why you never want to multitask when it comes to emails." She was interviewing a candidate for a leadership position and emailed a question to HR—or so she thought. It went to me instead!

   Some email errors can have more serious implications. Consider what happened at the *New York Times* a few years ago, as the Associated Press reported:

   > The New York Times *thought it was sending an email to a few hundred people who had recently canceled subscriptions, offering them a 50 percent discount for 16 weeks to lure them back. Instead, Wednesday's offer went to 8.6 million email addresses of people who had given them to the* Times.

3. **Include a signature block**, providing your reader with some information about you. Generally, this would state your full name, title, the company name, and your contact information, including a phone number. People have said to me: "Why is he making me search for his number? I hate that!" You also can add a little publicity for yourself, but don't go overboard with any sayings or artwork. Use the same font, type size, and color as the rest of the email. One engineer wanted her name to stand out, so she used 24-point, bright blue type. The rest of the email was 12-point black type. Her name stood out, but not in a good way.

4. **Don't overuse "reply all."** Too often, this only contributes to email overload. People don't want to receive emails that they don't need to see. It wastes their time. Use "reply all" only when it is necessary for *everyone* on the list to see the email.

5. **Don't send an email when you are angry.** In angry mode, you are likely to write unkind or nasty comments. Before you hit the send button, consider what the consequences of your words might be.

Put the email aside until you calm down. Then reread what you have written, and decide whether you really want to send those comments.

6. **Tell the sender if you received an email in error.** Unless you do, the person who sent the email will believe it was delivered to the correct person. A simple reply to the writer is all that is needed, such as: "I don't think you intended to send this to me. Just wanted to let you know."

There are several other elements of an email that merit their own chapters. Suggestions about subject lines can be found in Chapter 12, information on salutations is in Chapter 13, and you will find information on closings in Chapter 14.

QUESTION TO CONSIDER

Q. *What's the difference between CC and BCC?*

A. *CC* stands for "carbon copy" — the term refers to how copies were made in the days of typewriters — and it is used to send a copy of your email to everyone whose address you enter on that line. All the addresses are visible, so everyone who receives the email knows who else is receiving it. Only CC people with a need to know what is in your email. If not, you are adding to email overload.

BCC stands for "blind carbon copy," and it works in much the same way except that the email addresses on the BCC line are not visible to anyone except the sender. Recipients of the email do not know who else has received it. BCC inhibits open communication, so use it only if there is a good reason, such as respecting your recipients' privacy.

PRESCRIPTION FOR SUCCESS

Remember my acronym AIL. AIL stands for "address in last." Use this acronym to remind yourself not to send an email before you have finished writing and proofing the message. You can't send an email without an address. Even when you are replying to a message, it's a good precaution to delete the recipient's name and reinsert it only when you are sure the message is ready to be sent.

11. What's in an Email Address? A Lot!

I haven't opened emails—that later turned out to be from people I do business with—because I thought the emails were spam based on their addresses. I missed some important information.

A director of a national organization expressed this frustration after my talk on etiquette at a recent conference.

Your email address is important. It can convey a lot of information about you, including your name and where you work, and even your age range—for example, many assume that any email with an aol.com address probably belongs to a boomer.

The goal of a good address is to identify you to the recipient and to have that person open your email promptly.

If you are employed by a company, you will use its address format for work. But most people have additional email accounts that they use for personal communication and certain work-related business, such as a job search. Other individuals may be in business for themselves, or they may be recent graduates who need a professional address to connect with the world.

Take note of these tips before choosing your email address:

1. **Use your name in your email address.** People will know immediately who has sent the email. Use either your full name or your first initial and last name. Avoid using just initials. People may not recognize that "TDH" stands for "Tom Dick Harry."

2. **Do not use a cutesy name in business.** Yes, there may be exceptions if you are in marketing or an unusual field, but in most business situations, using something like "sexydiva1109@" sends an unprofessional message.

3. **Get creative if your name is already taken.** You may need to add your middle name, middle initial, or a number to your name.

4. **Be consistent with your address.** Some people have multiple addresses, using myriad variations of their names in them. It can be confusing to others if one day you are sjones@ and the next SusanJonesSmith@. Also, if you are no longer a student, it's time to replace your university address. You want to be recognized, and your new or potential colleagues may not know that you are abc@xyzuniversity.edu.

5. **Let people know if your email address changes.** Send an email to everyone on your mailing list and update your social media sites.

PRESCRIPTION FOR SUCCESS

Have your own domain. If you are in business for yourself, consider using your business name as your domain. For example: Tom.Jones@xyzconsulting.com. It lends substance to your business. If you don't yet have a business, consider claiming your name as a domain, anyway, to secure it for the future.

12. Grab Your Reader's Attention: Effective Use of Email Subject Lines

Can you send me some suggestions about email subject lines that work?

I was asked this question by a reporter who wanted to do an article on how to craft an effective subject line. The reporter was on to something: Most people will not open an email unless the subject line indicates it contains information worth reading.

You want your subject line to be descriptive, informative, and inviting—and to target your reader. Use just a few key words. And check carefully to eliminate any typos.

But the most important point about subject lines is to make sure you have one! Emails that have no subject line are less likely to be opened.

So what makes a good subject line? The obvious answer is that any subject line that entices your recipient to open your email is a good one. Here are some suggestions for achieving that:

1. **Provide a brief overview of the email content**, such as "Completed contracts" or "Update on budget."

2. **Remind people of something**, such as "Follow-up to our meeting" or "Deadline approaching" or "Next steps for the project."

3. **Start with the word *Question*,** such as "Question concerning my invoice" or "Question about the new software." You can also use "Quick question" for someone you know. And you can ask a question, such as, "Want 15% off your next sale?"

4. **Offer suggestions**, such as "Ideas for our upcoming roundtable." Or "This might boost your bottom line."

5. **Name a reference known to both of you**, such as "Jacob Jones suggested I contact you" or "Jen Smith asked me to contact you." Do not mention the name of someone you don't know, or the name of someone who will mean nothing to your recipient.

6. **Give useful information**, such as "7 tips for powerful presentations" or "An idea you might like."

7. **Provide a call to action**, such as "Sign up today: Volunteers needed for food drive" or "Action needed: Your contract is expiring."

8. **Communicate positive news**, such as "Good news about the project" or "Extra tickets available for conference."

9. **Express gratitude.** You can use "Thank you" or simply "Thanks" when emailing a thank you note.

10. **Say something unexpected**, such as "Relocating to our Dublin office!" (Of course, you would write this only if it were true.)

QUESTION TO CONSIDER

Q. *Do you use punctuation in a subject line?*

A. Subject lines do not need a period. You can use a question mark if your subject line is a question, and you can use an exclamation mark *sparingly*.

PRESCRIPTION FOR SUCCESS

Take note of subject lines that have caught your attention. You can often model yours on those successful examples. However, be careful not to echo subject lines frequently used on spam emails. Check your spam folder to see which catchy phrases are currently being used.

13. In the Beginning . . . Salutations Set the Tone for Emails and Letters

My name is spelled correctly in my signature block; why do so many people misspell it in the salutation?

Only my good friends call me Bobby—my coworker should use "Robert" or "Bob" in the salutation.

I hate reading an email that starts with "Good morning" when it is 9 o'clock at night. The writer has just highlighted that I am 12 hours behind in answering my emails.

Unfortunately, the salutation—whether in an email or a letter—provides endless ways to upset your reader, as indicated by these comments from participants in my seminars. And if you offend someone in the first line, that person may not read any further.

Here are suggestions for starting your correspondence without offense:

1. **Spell the recipient's name correctly.** Let me repeat this: *Spell the recipient's name correctly*. It may not bother you to have your name spelled wrong, but I want to impress upon you that many people are insulted if their name is misspelled. Check for the correct spelling in the person's signature block. Copy and paste the name to make sure you are spelling it correctly. Checking the "To:" line is also a good idea, as people's first and/or last names are often in their addresses.

2. **Don't shorten a person's name or use a nickname unless you know it is okay.** Use the person's full name ("Hi, Jacob") unless you know it is okay to use the shorter version (Jake). My name is Barbara, but please don't start your emails to me using "Hi

Barb." (And the only people who may refer to me as Babz are my son and his friends!)

3. **Avoid "Dear Sir/Ms."** This salutation tells your reader that you have no idea who that person is. Why then should the reader be interested in what you have to say?

4. **Use a non-gender-specific, nonsexist term** if you don't know the person's name. You can use Dear Client, Customer, or Team Member. You can also use Representative, and add it to any company name or department name, such as "Dear Microsoft Representative," or "Dear Human Resources Representative."

5. **Salutations are recommended in emails.** Email doesn't technically require a salutation, as it's considered to be memo format. When email first appeared, many people did not use salutations. Eventually, people starting adding salutations to appear friendlier and to soften the tone of their writings.

There is a hierarchy of greetings, from informal to formal, and you should match the salutation to the relationship you have with the recipient. The hierarchy follows this format:

Hi, / Hi Anna, / Hello, / Hello Julianna, / Dear Justin, / Dear Mr. Jones,

If the person you are writing to is a colleague, "Hi Anna," should be fine. If you don't know the person, or the person has significantly higher rank than you have, you may want to use the more formal greeting: "Dear Justin," or "Dear Mr. Jones."

In addition to the greeting, pay attention to these points:

- After two or three emails have gone back and forth on the same email string, the salutations can be dropped.

- The punctuation completing the greeting is a comma.

- If more than one person will receive an email, use "Hello Sara and Bill," or "Hello Everyone."

- "Hey" is a very informal salutation ("Hey Josh,") and generally should not be used in the workplace. Opening with "Yo" is definitely not okay, no matter how informal your relationship with the recipient. Use "Hi" or "Hello" instead.

- As illustrated in one of the opening quotes, there are people who don't like receiving an email that starts with "Good morning" or "Good afternoon." Although I believe this is a minor offense, using "Hello" instead eliminates the possibility of offending anyone.

6. **Salutations are required in letters.** In today's workplace, a letter is a more formal type of correspondence and should start with "Dear" followed by either the person's first name and a colon— "Dear Marie:"—or an honorific and the person's last name, followed by a colon—"Dear Mr. Jones:"

QUESTION TO CONSIDER

Q. I am uncomfortable using "Dear" in my salutations. Do I have to use it?

A. Yes, in a letter, you do. I know that "Dear" is a very endearing word to some people, and they have a difficult time applying it to colleagues or strangers. I understand the feeling. Nevertheless, I encourage people to follow this writing guideline and use "Dear" in the salutation.

PRESCRIPTION FOR SUCCESS

Drop the honorary title (Mr. or Ms.) if you are unsure of a person's gender. Instead, use the person's first and last names:
- "Dear Chris Williams" for gender-neutral names
- "Dear PJ Jones" if the person uses initials instead of a first name
- "Dear Hongbo Tan" for an international name with which you are not familiar

14. Saying Goodbye:
Suggestions for Closing Your Emails

If customers include a closing in their emails, it indicates to me that they are friendly, and so I will do their work first.

A woman in one of my writing classes made this comment when we were discussing how to end an email. Others joined in and added that they liked seeing closings in emails they received.

I agree. Emails that simply end without some kind of closing can seem too abrupt.

During my classes, numerous questions surface about which closing is appropriate in our casual workplace. Deciding what to use can be confusing. When email first appeared in the workplace, salutations or closings were rarely used. Over time, we have added both to our emails. Though there has been some discussion in the media lately about whether we need to use closings, in my experience, the majority of people want to keep them.

I encourage businesspeople to use closings. Here are my suggestions:

1. **If you start with a salutation, end with a closing.** It provides balance to the email.

2. **Match the closing to the salutation.** If you use an informal salutation, such as "Hi Amanda" or "Hello Gavin," use "Regards," "Best," "Best regards," "All the best," or "Thanks," to close. If you use a more formal salutation, such as "Dear Ms. Jones," use "Best regards," or "Sincerely." Only the first word of the closing is capitalized, and the closing is followed by a comma.

3. **With no disrespect intended, avoid using "Respectfully."** This very formal closing is usually reserved for government officials and clergy. Another closing to avoid is "Faithfully yours." This wording comes from British English, and a woman from India who was in

my class said that she was advised very quickly by her boss not to use that closing in the United States.

4. **End with a "closing statement."** Since closings are more relaxed in emails than in letters, you can use a brief statement as your closing, such as "See you at the meeting" or "Thanks for your help."

5. **Once emails become a back-and-forth conversation, you can drop the closing.** It begins to sound repetitious and somewhat silly if you have a long string of emails all proclaiming, "Best regards, Mike."

PRESCRIPTION FOR SUCCESS

You can use the closing to tell people what you want to be called. On the line under "Best" or "Regards," type your name the way you want to be addressed. If you want to be called "Mike" instead of "Michael," you should sign "Mike."

15. Reasons You Make Mistakes in Email, and Proofreading Solutions

"I don't proof my emails until after I hit send," a young woman told me during a recent business writing class. "I just want the email off my desk. It's too nerve-racking otherwise." I was startled. After I thought about her comment for a moment, however, I realized that she was not unique in this behavior. Others in my writing classes have expressed similar sentiments, though they may not have phrased them quite so bluntly.

"Proofing after sending" is a pointless exercise, but it's only one of the reasons that people have mistakes in their writings that could be fixed easily. Others include these four:

1. **Typing and walking.** If you don't want to run into walls, people, or traffic, you need to concentrate on your surroundings when walking. It is difficult to look where you are walking and type an email at the same time, so it's tempting to skip any proofing. Don't walk and type!

2. **Not paying attention to spelling and grammar suggestions provided when writing email.** Spell-checkers and grammar guides available on your computer or phone do not replace your good brain, but they may catch many of your errors.

3. **Not reviewing the corrections made by autocorrect.** One man told me he meant to say "Sorry for the inconvenience," but autocorrect changed the sentence to "Sorry for the incontinence." Big difference!

4. **Not realizing the impact mistakes can have on your career or reputation.** No one is perfect, and anyone can make a mistake occasionally, but if you make mistakes frequently, or have a number of them in any one email, your reputation is likely to suffer, and the professional consequences could be serious.

Proofreading Suggestions

- Read your message out loud *syl-la-ble by syl-la-ble*. This is the best way to catch your errors. If you read the words slowly, you are more likely to notice any missing words, wrong words, misspellings, and wrong tenses of verbs. The reading should be done *slow-ly*, so you really pay attention to each word. If you speak quickly, you may get caught up in the meaning of your words and miss the mistakes. As one engineer in my class said, "Unless I read slowly, I am reading what is in my head, not what's on the screen."

- Learn your common errors. These are the mistakes that you regularly make. When you know your typical errors, look for them.

- Double-check any numbers. This is just good common sense. A misplaced decimal point can be very costly.

These suggestions will add only seconds to the time you spend on an email, and they will help you catch many of your errors. Isn't your reputation worth those few moments?

Exercise

Read the following paragraph to yourself and count the number of errors. Then read it again slowly, *syl-la-ble by syl-la-ble*. Did you catch any additional mistakes?

Joyce Hoff, my office manger, will be sending you a email this week. We had discuss a couple of different design for you two days of training. Can we talk this week to finalize the design?

Turn to page 43 to see if you caught all the errors.

Answer

Here is the corrected paragraph for the Exercise on page 42.

Joyce Hoff, my office manager, will be sending you an email this week. We had discussed a couple of different designs for your two days of training. Can we talk this week to finalize the design?

PRESCRIPTION FOR SUCCESS

Follow the "look for one" rule. When you are proofreading, expect that you will find at least one mistake. Don't stop looking until you have found one, or are quite satisfied that there are no more to find. It's easy to miss errors unless you have a strategy for finding them.

16. How Do I Become a Better Writer? Let Me Count the Ways . . .

A man in my writing class kept a diary and wrote in it every day for 15 years. He wrote after work, about work. He filled one notebook a year. He recently reviewed the notebooks and was amazed to see how things have changed at his workplace—and how much better his writing has become!

Writing is not a skill that comes naturally to everyone. Yet you don't have to be a professional writer to write a successful email. Your writing, like any other skill, can significantly improve with a solid understanding of the process, and with lots of practice.

In addition to following the writing suggestions already provided in this section, here are two key ways to help you become a better writer. As author Stephen King said, "If you want to be a writer, you must do two things above all others: Read a lot and write a lot."

1. **Read.** The more you read, the better your writing will become. Notice how the writer uses words. Was the document easy to read? Was there any unusual word usage? Did you learn anything new about writing? I remember discovering the word *conundrum* in an article and thinking, "What a great word. I need to use it." And I have.

2. **Write.** It sounds simple, but it's true: The more you write, the better your writing becomes. Keep a diary. Start a blog (see Chapter 18). You also can volunteer to write articles for your company or community organizations. The content of your writings is less important than having an opportunity to practice putting your thoughts into words.

These additional tips are also helpful:

3. **Have a writing buddy.** Choose someone you trust, and together you can help improve each other's writings. How? You proof your buddy's documents, and he or she proofs yours. It is easier for other people to catch your mistakes, as they are reading what you've written with fresh eyes.

4. **Take a class or attend a seminar.** Many colleges offer writing classes through their continuing education programs for adults, and many companies provide writing seminars to their employees as part of the training curriculum. By participating, you will learn more about the writing process, get to practice writing in a supportive environment, and receive feedback on your writings.

PRESCRIPTION FOR SUCCESS

Acquire an up-to-date style manual, and use it. These manuals generally explain the rules of grammar and punctuation, and even offer writing guidelines. Chances are some guidelines on grammar or punctuation have changed since you learned them, and unfortunately some of us never learned many rules in the first place. Use the manual as your handy reference, and look up any questions you have.

Examples of well-regarded manuals, some with subscription websites, are:

- *The Gregg Reference Manual* (mentioned elsewhere in this section)
- *The Elements of Style* by Strunk and White
- *The Chicago Manual of Style*
- *The Associated Press Stylebook*

They differ in the amount of information contained, organization of the content, and interpretation of some of the rules. Review a couple of these resources and then choose one you like, or the one your company recommends.

Be cautious if you rely on Google to answer your questions. Some of the sites providing answers may be professional, others not so much. Also, you may sacrifice consistency, since you will probably use a different reference or site each time. For example, one site may tell you to spell *internet* with a capital *I*, but another may recommend a lowercase *i*. The key is to choose one resource or site, which will help you to be consistent throughout your documents. (Of course, if your boss wants you to use a certain version, use it.)

17. "It's What You Wrote!"
How Facebook, Twitter, LinkedIn, and Others Can Kill Your Career

A former student asked me to review his LinkedIn page. Unfortunately, he had misspelled his job title ("Assistant Communication Coordinattor"). When I mentioned this to a colleague, he said that such typos could affect the student's ability to get hired.

A woman in my class said that when her church was publicizing an upcoming event on its Facebook page, an administrator wrote: "Worship at Rev. Jones." She explained, "It should have said: 'Worship with Rev. Jones.' Using the preposition 'at' instead of 'with' made the Reverend a God." She was embarrassed that no one had proofread the post and caught the error.

I received the following direct message on Twitter: "Im a freshman and im definitely gonna need business etiquette skills in the future." I agreed!

Social media has significantly influenced the ways we can communicate and interact with others. What hasn't changed is the importance of writing effectively. You don't want to make embarrassing mistakes that undermine your professionalism.

LinkedIn, Facebook, and Twitter all deal in written content, with some allowing more text than others. When sharing on social media, remember these writing suggestions:

1. **Always assume the quality of your writing matters.** As illustrated above, there are consequences to making errors. Proofread your writings before you post anything. I know that social media can spur quick commentary, but at the very least, read your comments

out loud before you post. It will take just a few seconds, and you will catch many of your errors.

2. **Be mindful of what you choose to write about.** You never know who may see your comments. Posts can quickly go viral.

3. **Understand that what you write in the comment section under articles or posts is also part of your professional image.** This applies to comments on social media as well as on news sites, such as the *New York Times* and the *Huffington Post*. Comments with typos or crass wording cost you credibility.

4. **Don't try to solve complex issues on social media.** When the issue gets complicated or the topic is touchy, stop writing and call the person, if you can. And if you don't know the person, stop participating in the conversation.

5. **Follow these specific tips for the major sites:**

   • **Facebook.** Many people have a personal Facebook page, and often people forget that it can impact their careers. Your colleagues, bosses, and prospective employers may check your page. Though visual content is the major part of most posts on Facebook, there are some writing concerns. If you use strong negative language, put people down, name-call, or curse, what are you saying about yourself? And why would I want to work with you?

   Remember that what you post may come back to haunt you. One of my students summed it up well:

   A friend of mine was in a bad car accident and is seeking reimbursement for her medical expenses. I know that she was in a lot of pain and saw many doctors. However, if you were to read her Facebook page, it would appear that she has been having a grand time since the accident.

   • **LinkedIn.** This is the social network for business professionals, and your profile will be checked by colleagues as well as prospective employers. Grammarly (a grammar website) studied 100 LinkedIn profiles in the consumer packaged goods industry and found that professionals whose profiles contained fewer mistakes also achieved higher positions. Make sure you have someone proof your profile. If you are uncomfortable writing your own profile, hire an expert. There are many professional résumé writers who provide this service.

You can also publish on LinkedIn. Many people post their blogs on the site. LinkedIn does not provide editors to proofread this content, and unfortunately, I have seen many typos in articles and comments.

- **Pinterest.** Pinterest contains mostly visual material, but typos in your profile can destroy your credibility. My intern helped with my Pinterest content. She was great at titles, but I had to remind her to proof the board and pin descriptions. Typos were not okay.

- **Twitter.** The goal of Twitter is to engage with your followers. One of the people I coached in the past wrote: "I feel as if we talk often because I read your Twitter feed regularly." The main writing sections are your short profile and your individual tweets. Even though tweets are limited in length, I suggest leaving room for your tweet to be retweeted. Use correct punctuation, including periods, commas, and apostrophes. Start each tweet with a capital letter, and avoid using all caps—this comes across as shouting. If you share a photo, pay attention to the writing in the caption. Use a hashtag (for example, #Proofread) that indicates your topic. This helps to categorize your content and allows you to engage in the discussion.

PRESCRIPTION FOR SUCCESS

If you haven't proofread your profile and other statements on your social media sites, or haven't reviewed them in a while, do so now. You may be surprised at the mistakes you find.

18. Improve Your Writing—and Reputation—Through Blogging

The recruiter was really impressed that I blog.

My writing has significantly improved since I started blogging.

People have thanked me for my blogs!

My health blog has helped me establish my personal-training business.

Many people blog, and some people have become famous as a result. (Think author Julie Powell's blog, based on duplicating the recipes in one of Julia Child's well-known cookbooks. It became the focus of the 2009 movie *Julie & Julia* starring Amy Adams and Meryl Streep.) Others have made money by advertising on their sites, and some people have made blogging their full-time jobs.

But that is not what this chapter is about.

This chapter discusses the importance of blogging as a way to improve your writing. As mentioned numerous times in this book, if you want your writing to improve, you have to write, and blogging provides a forum for you to do that.

Of course, there are additional career benefits to blogging. You can enhance your reputation by becoming known as an expert on the subjects you choose to discuss. A well-presented and interesting blog also may help you stand out from the crowd when you look for a new job or career.

Follow these suggestions to write an effective blog:

1. **Choose a main area of focus.** And make sure you are passionate about the topic. Your enthusiasm will come through in your writings. You don't need to be *the* expert, but you do need some

knowledge about your subject, and you also must be willing to research what you don't know. Select a name for your blog that conveys your focus. My blog, *Pachter's Pointers: Business Etiquette Tips and Career Suggestions*, clearly defines what I write about.

2. **Follow your company's guidelines.** Many companies have policies about what you can and cannot discuss on your personal blog. For example, you would not want to write about any confidential or proprietary information, among other things. And remember that your blog is not private. You never know who may see your comments.

3. **Write for your reader.** Identify the kinds of people you think will be your readers. What do they know about your topic? What do they *want* to know about your topic? What insights and information can you provide for them?

4. **Choose a creative title for each post.** You want your title to attract readers and also to appear on search engines. If you include words that are key to your topic, your blog should pop up when people search for those key words. For example, if you are writing a blog about rules for email, your title might be "Email Rules: Don't Drive Your Readers to Distraction." Some readers may respond to a question: "Giving a Presentation? Ways to Answer Questions like a Pro." You also can give your readers an idea of what they will learn: "How to Avoid Mistakes in Your Writings."

5. **Make your blog easy to read.** Write well. Follow the suggestions provided in this section. Use short paragraphs, vary the length of your sentences, and use headings and lists. You need to proofread your writings and have someone else look at your blog before you post. Typos and errors can destroy your credibility.

6. **Include other resources.** If possible, include images, add links to other relevant blog posts and articles, and also mention research or quotes by well-known individuals that support your positions. These additions help build your credibility.

7. **Start with a good opening.** You want to grab your readers' attention and encourage them to continue reading. There are numerous ways to do this, including using a question, telling a story related to your post, or using quotes. This chapter starts with quotes, for example.

8. **Set a schedule for writing and posting.** And stick to it! Decide how often you will post—every month, every two weeks, every week? When you set a schedule, you are more apt to keep it. Plus, your readers will know when to expect your commentary.

9. **Enable comments.** Allow people to write comments on your blog. You can ask a question at the end of the blog to encourage people to contribute, such as: "Have you ever experienced anything like this?" "What tips would you add?" or, simply, "What do you think?"

10. **Promote your blog.** Post your blog on your social media sites, including your Facebook page, your LinkedIn page, and your LinkedIn groups. Tweet the blog to your followers. Encourage people to subscribe to your blog by including a link for them to provide their email addresses. Include share buttons, which will allow your readers to share your post with their followers. Put your blog address in your personal email signature block. Some well-known business sites, including *Business Insider* and *Entrepreneur*, may accept your blog for publication. Go to their sites and follow the guidelines for becoming a contributor.

PRESCRIPTION FOR SUCCESS

Don't hesitate—start a blog! There are many blog platforms that make this easy to do. A lot of people use WordPress, which is a free blogging platform. Go to wordpress.com and follow the instructions. Blogger (blogger.com) is also a popular platform. There is much more advice available, both on the web and in books, to help you with your blog, including suggestions for monetizing it.

19. Texting for Business? It Is Still Writing!

A woman texted her boss that she didn't feel well and wouldn't be at work. Then she turned off her phone. Her boss needed to ask her for information on an order due that day but couldn't reach her. He was annoyed that she had texted him instead of calling, as he could have asked her for the data.

Texting can be a very quick, unobtrusive way to communicate with others. Yet it needs to be done professionally when used for business. As the above comment indicates, there are opportunities to mess up. For instance, if you have important information to convey, you need to make sure it has been received.

Keep the following suggestions in mind when texting for business:

1. **Pay attention to your tone.** Be careful that your comments don't sound more strident than you intend. If you write in complete sentences, your texts likely will sound less abrupt. Read your message out loud. If it sounds harsh to you, it will sound harsh to the recipient. Humor is difficult via text, and sarcasm doesn't work.

2. **Be polite, especially with customers.** Politeness helps to convey a pleasing tone. It makes you seem friendly and gracious. Start your text with "Hi," and end with "Thanks" when appropriate. Also, add "please" before you request something, as in "Please respond by noon."

3. **Keep your texts straightforward.** Don't address complicated or time-dependent topics in texts. For complex issues, put your comments in an email, or call the person involved. Speaking directly to the other person is especially important if your message involves tight deadlines or a change in meeting times or locations. Texting

is also too casual a medium for conveying bad news. And—you wouldn't think I would have to say this, but I do—don't quit your job via text.

4. **Is texting the preferred method?** The general guideline is that if someone texts you, you should reply by text. If someone emails you, you should reply by email. It's important to know what your recipient prefers—maybe it's a phone call. Using a person's preferred method helps ensure that your message is received. Most workplaces use a variety of communication modes. Also, some organizations may use texting for specific purposes, such as colleges sending alerts to their students or companies updating customers on their services.

5. **Use abbreviations cautiously.** If you are going to use the texting shorthand known as txt-spk (or by various other names), make sure the shortcuts you use are appropriate for your readers. It is generally best not to use these abbreviations when texting customers, clients, potential customers, bosses, and vendors. Your customers may not know that BRB stands for Be Right Back. Or they may not like that you are being so casual with them. And never use abbreviations that convey curse words, such as WTH or WTF—which I won't define here.

6. **Double-check that you are texting the correct person.** It's possible to send a text message to the wrong person—just like in email. A salesperson thought she was texting her assistant and bragged about her huge sale to a new customer, whose number she had just entered into her phone. She accidentally sent the text to the customer, who felt exploited.

7. **Know that autocorrect and voice-to-text features are not perfect.** These features can misinterpret words or phrases and change your message into totally different—often embarrassing—content. Reread your message before you send it, and make sure that the message you are sending is the message you intended to send.

8. **Use correct spelling and punctuation.** Your friends may not care about your spelling ability, but your customers do. If you misspell

words or use bad grammar, your customers are likely to question your professionalism.

9. **Don't text when others are speaking.** Texting under the table during a meeting is rude to the speaker and to the other participants. You may think that your actions are not visible, but your body language gives you away. This may not be a writing issue, but it is one of my pet peeves about texting. At the beginning of my seminars, I end my introductory remarks with, "And *p-l-e-a-s-e*, don't text under the table. I can see what you are doing, and it's distracting."

PRESCRIPTION FOR SUCCESS

Maybe you have read those surveys that say people would rather give up alcohol, chocolate, coffee, and even sex than give up their smartphones for a week. But in the workplace, do try to control that urge to be constantly texting or scrolling through your messages. Instead, look up and greet colleagues when you are walking down the hallway, riding in the elevator, or sitting in the cafeteria. Engage in conversation. You never know whom you might meet, or how a chance encounter may impact your career.

20. Don't Write That! The Top 10 Grammar Gripes (and Other Errors)

When I see a spelling error, I assume the person is lazy and didn't take the time to use spell-check.

I make negative assumptions about someone's intelligence when I get an email with grammatical errors.

One of the questions that I ask my class when we start our discussion on grammar and other writing errors is, "What are the mistakes you notice in other people's writings?" As they generate a list of various errors, they often make negative comments about the writers who made the errors, such as those quoted above.

Many of the same errors surface in every class. The list later in this section highlights the errors that show up most often on my participants' lists, along with some of the mistakes I find in those same participants' samples. So perhaps the moral of this chapter is twofold—assume people will make negative assumptions about you if you make frequent grammatical, spelling, or punctuation errors; and don't judge others' work unless you are sure your own is exemplary.

Eliminating errors is important, and your goal is clarity with accuracy. Most companies expect you to know the basic rules of grammar, punctuation, and word usage, and to follow them.

Some employees may be ahead of the curve in some of these areas. They may be tempted to show off their knowledge by using such words as *irregardless* because they know it is listed as a word (albeit nonstandard) in some dictionaries, or to substitute *they* as a singular pronoun for *he or she* because they know it is gaining acceptance from some language experts. Don't do it. Most people simply will think you are wrong and judge you accordingly.

Here are the top 10 gripes (grammar and otherwise) culled from numerous lists:

1. **Confusing sound-alike words.** Writers frequently confuse homophones, which are words that sound alike but have different spellings (usually) and meanings. Examples include:

   - **Your and you're.** *Your* is possessive. *You're* is short for "you are." Example: *You're* going to visit *your* best friend in Chicago.

   - **They're, their, and there.** *They're* is short for "they are." *Their* is possessive. *There* refers to a place. Example: *They're* all in *their* car, which is parked over *there*.

   - **Two, to, and too.** *Two* is the same as the number *2*. *To* is usually a preposition or the infinitive form of the verb. *Too* means also, in addition, or excessively. Example: She covered her ears with *two* hands *to* block the music, which was *too* loud.

2. **Having spelling errors.** Use spell-check every time, even if you are confident in your spelling abilities. Spell-check doesn't replace your good brain, but it's a helpful tool for catching many errors. (The red squiggly line under a word in Microsoft Word usually indicates a misspelled or unknown word.)

3. **Using the serial or Oxford comma inconsistently.** The serial comma is the one placed immediately before the conjunction *and* or *or* in a list of three or more items. How it's used stirs strong feelings among language lovers—and whether they are for or against it, most believe that their opinion is the *correct* opinion. Whichever side of the debate you fall on, use your commas consistently.

4. **Using personal pronouns incorrectly.** Many people use the wrong pronoun when they are speaking, which makes it easy to do so when writing, too. If you aren't sure, test your sentences. Some examples:

   - If you write, "Me and my friend went to the movies," drop "my friend" and say the sentence aloud: "Me went to the movies." Wrong! Instead, write "*My friend and I* went to the movies."

- The same test works for objective pronouns: "Kathy invited he and I to her party" becomes "Kathy invited he . . ." or "Kathy invited I . . . ." Both of these are wrong. Use "Kathy invited *him and me.*"

5. **Using "would of" instead of "would have."** Never write "would of" or "could of," as in "I could of gone to the meeting." This written usage probably came about because of how the spoken contractions sound: *could've* and *would've.* Correct usage is always "could have" and "would have."

6. **Placing periods and commas outside closing quotes.** In American English, periods and commas go inside the closing quotation marks, as in: She called out, "We're almost there." This is true even if the quotes enclose a title, as in: He read a passage from "Harry Potter and the Cursed Child." (British English is more complicated.)

7. **Using words that are not words.** Many people are horrified by the use of *anyways* and *irregardless*, or phrases like "whole nother" (instead of *another*) and "for all intensive purposes" (instead of "for all intents and purposes"). Writing them will make you sound uneducated. One student said, "When I hear someone say *irregardless*, I stop listening." But remember what we said earlier—language is always changing. Some dictionaries allow *irregardless* as a word, though they usually label it "nonstandard" or "colloquial."

8. **Abusing apostrophes.** Apostrophes are so often misused that the situation is sometimes called the apostrophe catastrophe. Remember that the apostrophe indicates possession—"the sailor's hat"—or marks missing letters in contractions—*haven't.* It doesn't indicate the plural form of a noun. Generally, adding an *s* makes a noun plural: "One dog met another, and both dogs ran off."

9. **Confusing subject/verb agreement.** The rule is simple enough—subject and verb must agree in number. So, a singular subject must be followed by a singular verb, as in "Humor is essential to success as a comedian." But not all sentences are so simple. A compound subject frequently takes a plural verb: "Charm and good looks

are essential for a career as a leading man." And there are many more complications, such as prepositional phrases: "Every one of the office staffers has his own cubicle." (One is the singular subject of has.)

10. **Being redundant.** This is a quite-common error that bothers many of my students, especially when it refers to time—as in, "6 p.m. tonight" or "8 a.m. this morning." Remember that *p.m.* stands for "post meridiem," or "after noon," and *a.m.* means "ante meridiem," or "before noon." Drop the "tonight" and "this morning" when you use *a.m.* and *p.m.* Oh, and remember: When the clock strikes 12, refer simply to *noon* or *midnight*.

PRESCRIPTION FOR SUCCESS

In addition to homophones (addressed in this chapter), words that sound similar and are commonly confused include *then* and *than*, and also *affect* and *effect*.

Try to remember that *then* generally refers to time, as in "We had lunch and then went to the movies." However, *than* is a conjunction indicating comparison, as in "His essay was better than mine."

Affect is usually a verb, meaning to influence something, as in "Budget cuts may affect how many people we can hire." But *effect* is usually a noun, meaning the result of something, as in "The team's loss had a negative effect on school morale." (There are exceptions to these generalities, but the usage outlined here applies to most situations.)

PART II

PRESENTATION SKILLS: TALK YOUR WAY TO THE TOP

The ability to make an effective presentation is an important business skill.

But numerous people have told me they would do anything to get out of speaking in front of an audience. Many tell me that even the thought of attending my class on public speaking makes them start to feel queasy!

As a presenter, you need to get your point across. And if you do so effectively, not only does your audience gain information, but you look good.

Yet many people, at all levels, are unsure how to appear confident and credible when speaking in front of others. Even seasoned professionals may stumble when it comes to speaking in public, which is why so many seek coaching to improve their presentation skills.

Whether you are a manager explaining new programs to your employees, a job seeker presenting in front of a prospective employer, or a vice president speaking to your board of directors, the information in this section will help you to achieve presentation success.

21. Presentation Panic—Take These Steps to Avoid Running off the Stage!

A couple of years ago, movie director Michael Bay made head-lines when he abruptly left the stage during his presentation for Samsung at the Consumer Electronics Show in Las Vegas. The video of his (very short) talk and sudden exit went viral.

Since public speaking is often listed as the number one fear that people experience, Bay's very public meltdown when his teleprompter failed could discourage others from making presentations.

But there are steps you can take that will allow you to continue with your presentation regardless of whether your teleprompter fails, your mind goes blank, or other difficulties occur. And then you can walk off the stage proudly, mission accomplished.

The most important response to an unexpected situation is to take charge. I tell my classes: "If you are not bothered by the mishaps that can and do occur, your audience will not be bothered either. It is when you get upset that your audience gets upset." It's really important to remember this.

Here are additional tips to help you maintain control of yourself and your audience:

1. **Don't rely only on a teleprompter.** This seems such an obvious point, but often people don't concern themselves with the technical aspect of their presentations. Have notes with you. You don't have to use them, but knowing they are there will help you to stay calm.

2. **Have backups of any materials or slides.** Keep these resources with you—don't trust them to somebody else. You also can store additional backups in the cloud, but make sure you know how to access them. Establishing your own fail-safe backup system is essential, but it is something that people often forget to do. When

I was speaking at a conference for 1,000 women in a distant city, the organizers wanted my slides ahead of time. I sent them, and they acknowledged receiving them. You might think I had nothing to worry about as a result—my presentation materials were safely where they needed to be. When I arrived at the conference, however, I discovered they had lost my slides. I could have panicked, but I had numerous backups with me!

3. **Check your equipment ahead of time.** Make sure everything is working correctly before the presentation. You are not always in charge of the audiovisual system, but you can, and should, check with the technicians who are.

4. **Mingle before the presentation.** When you can, go up to people, shake hands, introduce yourself, and welcome individuals to the presentation. This rapport-building helps people connect with you, and allows you to feel more comfortable with them once you are in front of the group.

5. **Acknowledge any technical difficulties and give the audience an alternative.** You could say something like, "I will take questions from you until the teleprompter is working again." Or "Since the teleprompter has stopped working, I will be using notes for a while." Or even "Discuss among yourselves for a few moments your experience with _____, while the technicians fix the equipment."

6. **Use a standard line.** Anticipate any difficult situations that you may encounter, and figure out what you will say if one of those situations occurs. You are less likely to panic if you have something to say. One speaker, when he forgets what he wants to say, will ask the audience, "If anyone has heard me speak before, what am I trying to say?" This line often elicits a laugh, and also gives him a couple of seconds to get back on track.

PRESCRIPTION FOR SUCCESS

Make presentations. The more presentations you make, the more comfortable you become. And they don't have to be work presentations. Any type of presentation will be good practice for you.

22. More Ways to Overcome Stage Fright

I'm just determined not to waste [hosting the Academy Awards] by being nervous. You want the buzz, but I prefer to think of it as excitement rather than nerves.
　　　—Hugh Jackman, actor, Academy Awards host, 2009

I get nervous when I don't get nervous. If I'm nervous I know I'm going to have a good show.
　　　　　　　—Beyoncé, entertainer

If these well-known and successful performers get nervous when appearing before an audience, what hope is there for the rest of us? Plenty! We can learn from their wisdom, and as their quotes indicate, you can embrace those nervous feelings to help you achieve success.

Here are some additional actions you can take to overcome your stage fright:

1. **Practice.** Of course, you are going to be nervous if you don't practice your presentation. The general guideline is to practice a presentation three to five times. And the key is to practice it out loud. You need to hear how the presentation sounds. Going over it in your head isn't good enough. Hearing the speech as your audience will hear it helps you to clarify the areas you need to work on.

2. **Have a "live practice."** In addition to practicing out loud, you want to have what I call a live practice. (Some refer to it as a dress rehearsal.) This is when you give your presentation as if you are giving it for real. To the degree that you can, dress for the presentation, have an audience, and give the presentation in the room you will be using for the real thing. This, then, becomes the first time that you give the talk, and for most of us, the first time is the toughest. You will learn what works well and what parts

need additional fine-tuning. Later, when you give the presentation for real, you will be more comfortable because you have already given it! One manager told me how she followed this advice: "I wanted a live practice, and so I had some of my employees listen to my new presentation during lunch. I provided food. It was really helpful."

3. **Follow my "92 percent rule."** Nobody's perfect, so why waste time chasing this elusive goal? This is why I came up with the 92 percent rule. Expecting perfection will make you hyper-focus on small errors, which can cause you to make more mistakes. Give yourself some wiggle room. If you are less than perfect, say 92 percent, you are still very effective—and that still rates an A in most classes.

4. **Tell yourself positive things.** How often have you said to yourself before a presentation, "I can't do this. I am going to fail." Or "Why the heck did I agree to do this?" Don't say these things! You are setting yourself up for failure. Tell yourself positive things instead, and you will start to believe them. I say to myself before every presentation, "I can do this. I can handle this."

5. **Do some exercises.** Athletes warm up before they perform, and you should, too. Most speakers feel their stress in the upper body. Exercises that will help you to loosen up—and dissipate stress—include the stretch-and-bend. Raise your arms and then lean forward to try to touch your toes. You also might try doing backstroke movements with your arms. These exercises should be done in your office or the restroom—not when you are on the podium waiting to be called on. Remember to breathe, and take some deep breaths. Many people, when they get nervous, tend to hold their breath.

6. **Pay attention to how food and drink affect you.** Know what caffeine does to you. Some people like the jolt it provides; others find it too much. Do not drink alcohol to calm your nerves. Know how various foods affect you. Some doctors say that milk may thicken your saliva, coating your throat and prompting much unappeal-

ing throat clearing. Stay away from soda and other carbonated drinks. Burping into your mic is not attractive!

7. **Ask yourself: Does the audience know I am nervous?** The audience does not know that you are nervous—unless you tell people you are or show them. So, don't! Follow the tips above, and continue reading through this section to learn how to project a confident and composed presence while you are presenting.

Exercise

Come up with two or three encouraging sentences that you will say to yourself before your next presentation. And remember, they must be positive. "I will not blow the presentation" is not positive. Instead, build up your confidence with upbeat lines such as: "It's going to be a good day" or "I'm prepared." Or choose words that are meaningful to you and repeat them to yourself with conviction.

PRESCRIPTION FOR SUCCESS

Don't discount yourself or your information in front of your audience. Avoid comments that belittle you or your talk. These include such statements as, "I hope this doesn't put you to sleep, but I want to talk about . . . ," or "I'm not really very good at public speaking," or "I didn't have a lot of time to put together the talk."

23. Don't Ramble: Use the Speech Organizer

I get overwhelmed when I start to put together a presentation.

I've heard this comment, in various incarnations, numerous times from participants in my seminars. It underscores just how many people find developing a presentation to be very challenging.

I agree; putting together a speech can be difficult—unless you have a clear understanding of how to proceed. That's where the Speech Organizer comes in (see graphic). It provides a visual representation of the parts of a speech and will help you organize your presentation and plan what you want to say.

The process starts by having you fill out each of the sections of the organizer with a few words that are relevant to what you want to say. Later, from this first step, you put together your presentation. As one woman said: "The flow of my speech was much better since I had a clear structure to follow."

But first things first. Here's how to fill out the Speech Organizer:

The Particulars

The first three items at the top of the organizer focus on the particulars of the presentation. You need to know the information that goes in these three segments before you can create an effective talk.

1. **The logistics.** Are you part of a panel or a stand-alone speaker? How much time do you have? Will you be using slides? Knowing the answers to these questions will help you decide how much information to discuss and how to present it.

2. **The audience.** Learn as much as you can about your audience before working on the presentation. As discussed in the next chapter,

SPEECH ORGANIZER

PACHTER & ASSOCIATES
THE EXPERT IN BUSINESS COMMUNICATIONS TRAINING

Logistics: Audience:

OBJECTIVE OF THE PRESENTATION:

INTRO-DUCTION

- Attention statement
- Purpose/objective
- Self-introduction
- Preview

BODY

Explanation/discussion (Three to five main points)

CONCLUSION

- Recap main points
- Memorable statement

Say "thank you" and take the applause!

the more you know your listeners, the easier it will be to answer their needs.

3. **The objective.** Knowing the objective of your presentation will keep you focused on your topic. If you are unsure or a bit hazy on what your objective is, complete this sentence to identify what you want your audience members to learn from your talk: "By the end of my presentation, the participants will . . ." And it should be just a sentence or two, expressed in clear language. If you write a paragraph or longer, you are most likely tackling too much for one presentation. For my talk on presentation skills, the objective is: "By the end of my presentation, the participants will know how to put together and deliver an informative presentation."

The Presentation

This section concentrates on the presentation and what you will cover in your introduction, the body of your talk, and the conclusion.

1. **Introduction.** During the introduction, you set the stage for the presentation. You let the audience know, in abbreviated form, what you will be discussing and why you are qualified to do so.

2. **Body.** During the body, you convey your information in a logical sequence. Identify and discuss your three to five main points and any subpoints you need to cover.

3. **Conclusion.** This is the time when you briefly recap what you discussed and end on a memorable statement—a story or quote or something similar that will make an impression. Your call to action would occur here also. This is when you want your audience to do something, such as sign up, donate, buy, or take some other action.

Afterward

After your conclusion, there are two more things to do.

1. **Say thank you.** The audience doesn't know that you are finished unless you say the words, "Thank you." Do not say, "Thank you for listening to me." It has been the audience's privilege to hear you speak.

2. **Take the applause.** I am sure you have seen speakers who have almost run off the stage and/or said, "Whew, glad that is over!" Do not do this. You should acknowledge the applause and walk off the stage or go back to your seat with your head held high.

PRESCRIPTION FOR SUCCESS

Once the Speech Organizer is filled out, you are on your way. From this structure, you create the presentation. See the following chapters for additional information on knowing the audience, completing the introduction and conclusion, adding stories, and writing the presentation.

24. It Would Have Been a Great Speech— for a Different Audience

I asked my boss for feedback after my first presentation to the executive team. He said it would have been a great presentation, except I hadn't paid any attention to the needs of my audience. Ouch!

A woman I mentor told me this story when I was doing research for this book. She said that unfortunately she learned the hard way the importance of knowing your audience.

You want your audience to relate to the content of your talk.

Years ago, I heard a story that I have never forgotten. The speaker said that he was asked to address an audience from Texas, so during his talk he made numerous references to oil or oil wells. Afterward, the organizer of the event asked him why he kept referencing oil. "Because you are from Texas," he said. "Yes," she replied, "but we are in cooking oil."

Before you begin to prepare your speech, find out as much as you can about your audience. The more you know about the people you'll be talking to, the more you can adapt your talk to their needs. How to discover their interests? Check with the person who asked you to speak, and for last-minute tweaks, mingle with audience members before the presentation. This doesn't mean you do a major overhaul of your talk, but it may allow you to reference a comment somebody made that reinforces a key point.

It is also important to answer these questions about your audience members:

1. **What do they know about your topic?** Is your audience composed of people in your field? Do they have a thorough knowledge of your topic do they have just a basic understanding, or are they

totally unfamiliar with it? Your answers will guide you in deciding how much background information to include and how technical you can be.

2. **What do they need to know?** Regardless of the composition of your audience, there may be some information that everyone needs to know. Make sure you cover that information.

3. **How much detail do people need?** The makeup of your audience often determines how much detail you provide. If the audience is composed of your colleagues, they may want to hear all the details. But if the audience is mostly members of upper management, they may want only a brief overview of your key points. This was my mentee's mistake—she gave her executive team more information than the executives wanted (or needed).

4. **What stories do you have that are relevant to your audience?** You want to make sure that the stories and examples you include are relevant to audience members. It adds to their understanding, and your credibility. (See Chapter 26 for additional information on how stories can enhance your presentations.)

5. **Are audience members attending voluntarily, or are they required to be there?** Sometimes people choose to attend a talk. In those instances, you usually can assume that they are interested in your topic. Other times, people may be required to attend your talk—which is often the case if it's part of a training session. You may choose to address that. During the introduction exercise, I often ask my seminar participants, "Why are you here—other than you have to be here? And I ask you that question in all sincerity, because to the degree that I can tailor this seminar to meet your needs, I will. But I need to know what those needs are." My participants are very responsive to this request.

6. **What questions are likely to be asked?** Think about what questions might surface, and know how you will answer them. It builds your credibility with your audience if you respond confidently to questions. (See Chapter 36 for more on answering questions.)

7. **Are any individuals likely to be hostile?** If so, when mingling before the presentation, make sure you interact with the potentially hostile audience members to help establish a connection. It's usually harder to be nasty with people you know. Also, during your introduction, stress your credentials. It's also harder to be confrontational with a true expert. And if there is a particularly difficult issue, you can bring up that objection before someone else does. You can say something like, "I know some of you are concerned about . . . . Let me explain how we will address that."

PRESCRIPTION FOR SUCCESS

When you address a group with different levels of knowledge of your topic, you can use the phrase, "As many of you know . . . ," and then make your point. This tells the experts that there is a reason for discussing this information, yet acknowledges that you know they know it already.

25. Openings and Closings Matter: Start with Strength, End with Impact

I didn't want to boast, so I never told the audience that I had a PhD in my subject. Maybe I should have. They started to question my credibility.

I never knew how to end my presentations. I just stood there and felt awkward.

These comments by seminar participants illustrate the importance of the introduction and conclusion to your presentation. You want to start a presentation with a powerful opening to grab your audience's attention, and then, after you have delivered your points, you want to close with an impactful statement so your message is remembered.

These goals are not as difficult to achieve as they may sound. The following general guidelines can be adapted to serve your presentation.

Introduction

As mentioned in a previous chapter, you set the stage for your presentation during the introduction. There are four components:

- **Start with an attention statement.** Your audience members walk into the room with their own thoughts in mind. You have to get them into your presentation quickly. Start with a compelling story, a quote, an illustration, an interesting statistic, an unusual news story that is related to your topic, and/or ask the audience a question. Do not start by saying "Today I would like to . . . ." You need to get your listeners' attention before you tell them what you'll discuss. I have started numerous presentation skills classes by quoting research that shows more people fear public speaking than fear death. To which Seinfeld adds, that means more people would rather be in the coffin than give the eulogy.

- **Tell the audience your objective.** During the introduction, let the audience members know what you are going to discuss. Don't assume that they know your purpose. Speak conversationally when you do, such as: "What I am going to discuss is how to put together and deliver an informative presentation." And mention how this will benefit the audience: ". . . so you can effectively convey your information to others."

- **Introduce yourself.** Self-introduction is the time to establish your credibility. If you are not introduced by somebody else, you need to introduce yourself. And this is not the time to be modest. Make sure the audience knows why you are qualified to talk about your topic.

- **Provide a preview.** Give a brief overview of your talk. This is the road map for your listeners, which makes it easier for them to follow you.

Conclusion

This section is similar to the introduction, but you don't need to discuss as many items. Your goal is to have the audience remember your talk. Include the following when wrapping up your speech:

- **Recap.** This is the time to review your key points. You don't want your audience to forget your comments.

- **Memorable statement.** You want the audience to think about your presentation after it has ended, so your closing needs to have impact. Take an approach that is similar to the "attention statement" in the introduction—use a compelling story, a quote, an illustration, or an interesting statistic that ties into your topic.

  I often end one of my women's seminars with a quote from the book *Key to Yourself* by Venice Bloodworth: "True happiness is a state of mind. And must come to you through recognition of your own power and the finding of your place in the world."

And then I add my final statement: "I would encourage you, as you leave here today, to continue to recognize your own power and to continue to find your place in the world. And I wish you well on that journey. Thank you."

Don't be afraid to be creative. Once, after a conflict class, a woman who had experienced a number of "aha!" moments asked if she could sing "Wind Beneath My Wings" (performed by Bette Midler in the movie *Beaches*) at the end of a three-day class. She had an incredible voice, got a standing ovation . . . and nothing more needed to be said to end the class.

QUESTION TO CONSIDER

Q. *Can you open a presentation with a joke?*

A. No, unless the joke is relevant to your topic and appropriate for business.

PRESCRIPTION FOR SUCCESS

Do not say, "In conclusion, . . ." as a lead-in to your ending. When people hear those words, they start packing up their belongings! You can say something like, "Let me wrap this up by saying . . . ," or "As we come to the end of our time together, I would like to finish with . . . ." This wording is not as abrupt, but still signals the ending of your talk.

26. Story Time: Use Tales to Engage with Your Audience

During one of our Sunday walks, my husband commented that I was interrupting him. I apologized. A few minutes later, he interrupted me. I asked, with a smile on my face, "How come I am not allowed to interrupt you, but you can interrupt me?" His response: "Is there a right answer to that question?"

A woman in one of my seminars told me about a delivery man who routinely walked into the office where she worked and greeted the women with "Hi, Hot Mommas." One of her coworkers told him: "Please don't call me 'Hot Momma,' regardless of whether I am or not." The next day, the man again visited the office and said, "Hi, Hot Mommas"—and then pointed to the woman who had confronted him and added, ". . . except for you."

My presentations include many anecdotes, and the examples above likely will find their way into some of my seminars. Good stories can reinforce and/or prove your key points. They create a picture for your audience, bringing to life the information you want to convey and making it much more memorable than a recitation of statistics or data.

Following the steps below will help you to add relevant stories to your presentations:

1. **View your experiences as opportunities to find stories.** Very few of my seminar participants forget my tale of tripping over the leg of a flipchart and falling down in front of a group of senior executives. I use it to illustrate the point that it's not what happens to you that matters; it is how you handle what happens to you. I got up, brushed myself off, and continued talking. Every story

doesn't have to be as extreme as my fall incident. You will soon build a reservoir of potential stories if:

- You observe something that illustrates a point in your presentation.
- Someone says, "That happened to me . . ." in response to some point you are making. That person's anecdote can add another voice to your information.
- You reference someone in an article or book, or on a website, who proves your point.

2. **Keep a story file.** Write down or copy just enough detail of the potential story so you will remember what happened. Keep this information in an electronic file or in an old-fashioned manila folder so the anecdote will be readily available.

3. **Prepare the story.** When you start to put your presentation together, go to your file and choose appropriate examples to support your points. Don't use someone's name unless you have the person's approval or the person is indisputably a public figure. Don't criticize or belittle anyone, and don't lie—but you can embellish the details a little for dramatic effect or to protect someone's identity. However, never embellish specific details, such as statistics. Tread lightly with humor. It can be effective, but it can also bomb badly. (Guidelines on using humor are in Chapter 33.)

4. **Practice.** In business presentations, shorter stories generally work best. Once you have chosen a story you want to use, practice saying it out loud, using as few words as necessary to convey your point. The more you include stories in your presentations, the more comfortable you become using them.

Exercise

To learn that stories can be all around you, choose one day to concentrate on your experiences. At the end of the day, review your interactions. Did you observe any interesting actions or hear any comments among your colleagues, bosses, clients, or strangers that are pertinent to your area of expertise? Write them down and add them to your story file.

PRESCRIPTION FOR SUCCESS

If something happens that would make a great addition to your story file, use your phone to record the highlights. If you wait until you get back to your office or computer, you may forget the story altogether.

27. Write the Presentation the Right Way

Everyone's speech was scripted and had been placed on the podium in advance. One speaker actually read someone else's speech, and he did not even notice!

I had written my notes on both sides of the paper, but I got nervous and never turned the papers over. Unfortunately, my speech didn't make a lot of sense!

There are many opportunities to mess up a presentation, as the two quotes above illustrate. Yet, creating effective notes can make delivering a presentation easier for you to give and easier for the audience to follow.

After you have filled out the Speech Organizer (see Chapter 23), the next step is to prepare your presentation. Here are the general steps:

1. **Review the Speech Organizer.** Make sure you have filled in all the sections.

2. **Generate your content.** What information is needed to achieve your presentation's objective? What do you know about your topic? What do you need to research? Will you need to review old presentations (yours or others), and/or talk to people for more input? Check your story file (covered in the previous chapter) to decide what stories and examples you will use.

3. **Identify your presentation structure.** There are many ways to organize a presentation. Think about your topic and your audience, and then decide how you will structure your material logically. Some people may take their topics and divide them into smaller sections. You may choose to structure your talk using a time sequence, such as past, present, and future, or first step, second step,

and so on. Others may decide their presentations lend themselves to a problem-and-solution structure.

4. **Optional step: script your speech.** This step is included cautiously. When people script their presentations, they often read those scripts (as the first quote at the beginning of this chapter illustrates), instead of regarding them as preliminary aids. And more often than not, they read quickly, don't look at the audience, and as a result sound stilted. You do not want to do this. But for some people, scripting a talk helps with the flow of the information.

5. **Create a phrase outline.** Either from the Speech Organizer or from your script, create a phrase outline—a few words or phrases that are complete enough so you remember the whole thought. These phrases become the outline of your talk and your notes. You will practice from these notes. And each time you practice, say the concepts differently. You don't want to memorize your speech. If you do that and then forget a word, you will panic. I'm sure you have seen speakers with that look of horror on their faces, trying to recall the exact wording!

6. **Include transitions.** These are the words and phrases that move your audience from point to point. They form the bones of your presentation, and without them, your audience may have a difficult time following you. Examples of transitions include: "My next point . . . ," "Having described the first step, let's move on to . . . ," or "That brings me to my next concept, ..."

7. **Use full-size sheets of paper.** Prepare your outline on 8½-by-11-inch paper. Use larger type (14 or 16 point, depending on your eyesight) so you don't have to hold your notes. If you use note cards, you are likely to hold them, and then be tempted to play with them. You don't want to do this. Number your pages. And only write on one side of the sheet of paper. If you use your phone for notes, you can have similar difficulties, including giving the impression that you are playing with your phone.

8. **Practice.** Now that you have prepared your notes, it's time to practice giving the presentation. Remember to practice your presentation out loud.

PRESCRIPTION FOR SUCCESS

Make use of PowerPoint's handout page. If you are using slides, you can print the handout page as your notes. Use the "three slides on a page" format and write your key phrases on the lines next to each slide. You can also print out a page for each slide, if you prefer.

28. Polishing Your Delivery: Pay Attention to the Details

It's normal for me to gesture a lot when I talk. But I see people watching my hands, and I'm not sure whether they are listening to me.

You might have a great presentation, but how you deliver that presentation will determine whether your audience receives your message, whether your reputation is enhanced, and whether your talk has the intended impact.

Any public speaker delivers information both verbally and nonverbally. And research has shown, as the quote above indicates, that your nonverbals can overwhelm your words.

This chapter provides tips on how to use your body language, including the way you dress, to convey your message effectively.

1. **Pay attention to your posture.** Don't let your posture become a distraction to your audience—no swaying or twisting your body. Stand with your feet parallel, approximately four to six inches apart. The weight should be on the balls of your feet, not the heels. Do not lock your knees. Your posture should not be rigid. And when you are not gesturing, your hands can be down at your sides. A participant in one of my classes commented, "When I bring my hands together, I tend to grasp them, instead of letting them relax at my sides."

2. **Walk, don't pace.** Now, you are ready to walk a little. Walk purposefully. Take a few steps and then stop. Do not pace back and forth, which becomes a distraction to your audience.

3. **Get out from behind a podium, when you can.** Sometimes you are locked behind a podium because the mic is fixed onto the podium.

But when you can, arrange for a lavalier mic, which attaches to your clothing. It will give you the freedom to move around, enhancing your connection with the audience.

4. **Make eye contact.** This is one of the most important aspects of a presentation. It connects you with your audience. When people get nervous, their eyes have a tendency to scan the room, never really making eye contact with anyone. Don't stare people down, but do look at them.

5. **Use gestures appropriately.** It's important to use gestures; they bring your words to life. Keep your gestures above your waist, and directed out to the audience. The larger the audience, the broader the gestures. But don't keep repeating the same ones. Pointing your index finger is usually seen as an aggressive gesture. If you want to point, use an open palm with your fingers together.

6. **Be aware of your facial expression.** Generally, you want to have a pleasant facial expression when speaking, but you also want your expression to be consistent with your comments. If you are discussing bad news and you are smiling, what will the audience members think? They might decide that you are unfeeling or not to be believed. The same is true if you are talking about good news and you are frowning.

7. **Dress for the presentation.** Your attire can help you come across as a self-assured person. Think about your audience members and what they will be wearing. Dressing slightly better than your audience adds to your credibility.

8. **Eliminate distracting behaviors.** The following mannerisms will bother your audience: Jiggling coins or keys in your pockets, drumming your fingers or wringing your hands, tugging or playing with hair (including a mustache), or clicking a pen. Wearing bracelets that make noise or earrings that sway when you walk also can divert attention from you.

Q. *My organization wants me to keep my name tag on all the time. Should I take it off for presentations?*

A. Yes. Your name tag becomes a visual distraction. You can remove it right before you speak and put it back on as soon as you are finished. I believe most organizations would accept this practice.

Exercise

You can't fix what you don't know you are doing. Record yourself when you can. The video feature on smartphones make this very easy. You can use a tripod to hold the phone, or prop your phone or tablet against something and record yourself that way. Review the recording and critique yourself. Analyze what you are doing with your posture, gestures, facial expression, and so on. Pick just one or two things to work on. When you are comfortable with those items, choose another problem area to hone.

PRESCRIPTION FOR SUCCESS

Do not put yourself down when you analyze your presentation skills or receive feedback from others. Many of us are very quick to do this. Improving your presentation skills is a process. Give yourself time, and encouragement, to improve.

29. Don't Put Your Audience to Sleep: Speak with Authority

She was monotone the whole time. I had to fight falling asleep.

My voice was steady, which made me seem confident, even though I felt nervous.

These quotes illustrate what a difference your voice can make to a presentation—it can either enhance it or turn it into a snooze fest.

My favorite example about the importance of voice is the story about author William Faulkner's acceptance speech for the Nobel Prize in 1950, which was recounted by biographer Joseph Blotner:

He stood too far from the microphone, his delivery was rapid and his Southern accent was difficult for most of the audience to understand. It was not until the next day when the text of the speech was released that the audience members realized they had heard one of the most memorable speeches they would ever hear.

Imagine—if Faulkner had not been so famous that the text of his speech was subsequently printed, a literary highlight might have disappeared.

You do not want your vocal features to prevent your audience from considering your comments. Here are some suggestions on how to use your voice to enhance your presentation and eliminate any boring monotone.

1. **Volume.** You need to speak loudly enough to be heard well. This point is subtle—you want not just to be heard, but to be heard so that what you say registers with your audience. Many people who speak softly don't realize that they do so, and some believe

that using a microphone will solve the problem. A mic certainly can help, but it will only ensure that your soft voice will be heard at the back of the room. You also want to speak with variety and vitality, so sometimes you will speak in a louder tone, and at other times you will want to project a little less volume.

2. **Rate.** Many people speak so quickly that it is difficult for an audience to follow. Open your mouth and pronounce all the syllables of your words clearly so people can understand you. (Don't overemphasize this, however, or you will sound silly!) Make sure you pronounce the endings of your words, as in the *-ed* in *expected* or the *-ing* in *expecting*. People often drop this last syllable as they blend their words together. And just as with volume, you want to vary your rate. Sometimes you may want to speak quickly, and other times slowing down will help to emphasize a point.

3. **Punch.** Vocally emphasize a word or phrase in your comments. When you write, you may do this by using italic font or underlining. When you speak, you punch it by stressing the word or phrase. This also adds vocal variety to your presentation. Consider this sentence: "Unbeknown to the speakers, the CEO came to hear their presentations." If you stress "the CEO," you can help convey the panic those speakers must have felt.

PRESCRIPTION FOR SUCCESS

Gain awareness of your voice image. Do you speak too quickly, or too softly? There is an easy way to evaluate your voice: Record a portion of a speech, and listen to how it sounds. Or when you leave a voice mail message for someone, listen to the message before you send it.

30. Eliminate Filler Words: *Um, You Know, Okay*

I noticed in presentations that some presenters used numerous filler words, which made their speech a bit harder to understand.

I counted 37 "okays" in his short presentation. It was not okay!

There are consequences to using filler words.

You don't have to be perfect. Nobody will notice an infrequent *um* or *okay*. We all use those words occasionally. But if the audience is counting the number of times you say *um*, they are not listening to what you have to say—and too many filler words make you appear unprepared and nervous, too.

Fillers words are simply extra words or sounds that we utter without thinking, but that muddle our sentences. After you record yourself practicing, you will be able to identify which ones you use and will start to notice them as you utter them. Before long, you'll be able to suppress them before they come out of your mouth.

But first you have to recognize whether you say *um*, *okay*, *all right*, *you know*, *er*, and/or *like*—probably the most common filler words used by American presenters. In Canada, you can add *eh* to the list.

Try these tips to help you recognize, and then eliminate, your filler words. As one participant in a class said: "Seeing the effect filler words had on my presentations, I want to eliminate them as much as I can."

1. **Record yourself.** When you can, record your presentations and identify any filler words you use. Count the number of times you use them. You may be shocked—or pleasantly surprised.

2. **Ask a trusted friend.** If you are not able to record your presentation, have a trusted friend or colleague in your audience identify and count your filler words for you.

3. **Be prepared.** The more confident you are with your material, the less likely you will be to hesitate and use filler words. One of my students summed it up best when he said: "I noticed I use the filler words *uh* and *um* when I am trying to complete my sentences. So in order to try and eliminate as many of them as I can, I have been preparing myself a little more than I did previously."

Exercise

Do this exercise in a private setting. Pick a simple topic, such as your house, car, or dog, and talk about it out loud for a few minutes without using the articles *the* and *an*. This exercise will force you to think about what words are coming out of your mouth before you utter them. You usually will notice your filler words as a result. But do not speed through the exercise: You want to hear each word. Over time, you will gain control of the flow of your words.

PRESCRIPTION FOR SUCCESS

Embrace the pause. People sometimes use filler words to fill a brief silence. But pausing can be an effective presentation technique. It allows you to get the audience's attention while also gathering your thoughts. The pause may seem like a long time to you, but usually it is just a few seconds — certainly not long enough for the audience to think anything is amiss.

31. Don't Let a Microphone Distract from Your Presentation

I have been asked to moderate a panel, and there's a chance I'll be holding a microphone. I'm a little nervous that my hand will shake. Do you have any suggestions?

A woman I had coached on presentation skills emailed this question to me.

She raised an important issue. How do you use a microphone so that it amplifies your voice but doesn't become a distraction, for you or the audience? You don't want your listeners to pay more attention to the microphone than to what you are saying.

Here are some suggestions for handling a microphone successfully:

1. **Arrive early at the meeting room** and practice using the microphone. Make sure the volume is set at an appropriate level.

2. **Consider your options.** These include:

   - If you are part of a panel and seated at a table with other panelists, your microphone probably will be placed on a stand. Since you don't have to hold it, you will be less likely to play with it.

   - If you are given a lavalier mic, it will be clipped to your clothing, so you won't have to hold anything. Remember to turn off this lapel mic when you are not presenting. (And never make critical comments about the event or other speakers, even if you think you are having a private conversation after the presentation. A number of politicians have been caught doing this while their mics were still on.)

   - If you are standing behind a podium that has a microphone mounted on it, you won't have to hold the mic. However, this is not an ideal place for a speaker to stand. You want to be able to walk around. If you can, use a lavalier mic.

3. **If you have to use a handheld mic,** experiment a little before your presentation to discover where you should hold the mic to get optimum volume and clarity. Do not gesture with that hand, or turn your head away from the mic to indicate a chart or screen—the people in the audience won't be able to hear what you are telling them. When you are listening to a question, or to other speakers, lower the hand in which you are holding the microphone.

PRESCRIPTION FOR SUCCESS

Remember that the more you worry about something—such as the possibility that your hand might shake while you are holding the microphone—the more likely you are to pay unnecessary attention to it. Chances are people won't notice the microphone unless you draw attention to it. Your audience wants to hear what you have to say. If you speak clearly and with confidence, you will have everyone's attention.

32. Are You Letting These Speaking Quirks Derail Your Presentation?

She giggles like a teenager. I find it hard to listen to her.

As you develop as a speaker, you should continue to fine-tune your presentation skills. The following three concerns tend to come up often. Though they are very different from one another, these speaking idiosyncrasies can sidetrack your audience, as one of these quirks did for the seminar participant quoted above.

1. **Be careful with absolutes.** These are words such as *always*, *never*, *all*, *everyone*, and *no one*. Speakers include them when they want their comments to apply to everyone in the audience. Yet in a business presentation, if you say something like, "I am sure everyone here panics before a presentation," there is usually someone in the audience who thinks, and may even say to others, that the statement is not true for him or her. You have then diverted the attention of that person—and maybe others—from your comments, and potentially derailed your presentation.

   Instead of using the absolute *everyone*, opt instead for *many here* or *almost everyone here*. The statement "I am sure almost everyone here panics before a presentation" still makes your point and feels inclusive, but acknowledges that there may be some who don't share this feeling.

   There are many other words you can use in your talks that are not all-encompassing, such as **probably**, *likely*, *most likely*, *often*, *fairly often*, *almost*, *almost always*, *rarely*, *very rarely*, *infrequently*, or *very infrequently*.

2. **Do not giggle.** Many people give a little giggle at the ends of their sentences, often involuntarily. By doing so, they diminish what they are saying. This giggle is an irritating mannerism that takes

away from the intended message. If you do it, you come across as childlike, not serious, or nervous about what you are saying. Both men and women giggle, but especially women—and many speakers don't realize they are doing it. It may be simply an expression of nervousness, but even if you are nervous, you don't want to convey that to your listeners. They will lose confidence in you.

3. **Beware of using buzzwords.** Every profession has its buzzwords and acronyms. You know what yours are. If you are speaking to your coworkers, they most likely will understand these words and know what the acronyms stand for. But if you are speaking to people in a different department, to people in your community, or to your customers, they may not know what you are talking about. When in doubt, leave the buzzwords out—or at least explain them.

PRESCRIPTION FOR SUCCESS

Don't simply declare that you don't have any vocal quirks, or that you don't use buzzwords—make sure. You may not be aware of how you sound to others. Listen to recordings of your talks with these points in mind, and find out if there are any problems you need to address.

33. Did You Hear the One About . . . ?
Guidelines for Humor

Thank you for pointing out my inappropriate humor. Though I strongly disagreed with you at the time, you were right. I began to notice people's reactions, and many seemed uncomfortable with my comments. I have since stopped telling jokes . . . and I just got a promotion.

I didn't realize that my use of humor was holding me back. Well, to be truthful, use of humor was one of a couple of items, but it was a big one.

One of these comments was made by a graduate student in one of my classes, and the other by a senior director whom I coached. But I have received many similar comments over the years. Employees at all levels can use humor poorly, and to the detriment of their careers.

Humor can serve to emphasize your points and also help people to remember them. But using humor poorly can diminish your message—and your reputation. If you are not comfortable with humor, don't force it. If you are going to use humor, keep the following in mind:

1. **Do not just tell jokes.** You are making a business presentation; you are not an entertainer. Only tell funny stories that enhance your comments. And remember, your stories must relate to your topic.

2. **Don't make jokes at anyone's expense.** You may insult your audience if you do. It's very easy to insult people without realizing it—you don't know whose grandfather worked where or whose mother did what. Besides, it's just not nice. You don't have to put people down to be funny. As comedian and talk-show host Ellen DeGeneres says: "Most comedy is based on getting a laugh at somebody else's expense. And I find that that's just a form of

bullying in a major way. So I want to be an example that you can be funny and be kind, and make people laugh without hurting somebody else's feelings."

3. **Stay away from any humor involving sex, politics, or religion.** These are controversial areas and can alienate the members of your audience—or at least make them uncomfortable.

4. **Use personal examples.** The best humor usually involves your own mishaps, as long as they don't put you down. Very few people ever forget my story of going to the bathroom during a seminar break with my lapel microphone on. One woman who heard me speak years ago came up to me recently and said, "Oh, you're the lady with the mic!"

5. **Use visuals.** Using an occasional funny photograph or cartoon can be amusing for your audience. Again, it must relate to your topic, and it should not be controversial. Just don't overdo your use of this technique.

Exercise

When you listen to other speakers, analyze their use of humor. What did they do to get the audience to laugh? Did they tell a story? If they did, why was it effective or ineffective? What can you incorporate into your next presentation?

PRESCRIPTION FOR SUCCESS

A relatively easy way to add humor to your presentations is to quote someone who said something funny. Just make sure you attribute the quote to the person who said it, and also that the quote is relevant to your topic. One of my quotes about presentation skills comes from the late comedian George Jessel: "The human brain starts working the moment you are born and never stops until you stand up to speak in public."

34. "He's Still Talking!" The Secrets to Managing Time When Presenting

My speech went over my allotted time. They hated me!

I panicked when I was told to add 10 minutes to my talk!

Participants in my presentation skills classes or coaching sessions often want to learn how to judge the timing of their presentations. I often hear comments similar to those quoted above. These students seem to have two major concerns:

- How do you calculate correctly how long your talk will take? Many people misjudge their timing, and either they go over their allotted time, or they run out of things to say.

- How do you quickly adjust the length of your talk? What do you do if you are told, shortly before you are to begin, that you have more time, or less, than you had anticipated?

The following suggestions can help you address the problems of timing:

1. **Prepare properly.** If you have prepared what you want to say, you are less likely to ramble, which would add additional time to your talk. You also are less likely to forget material, which would shorten your presentation.

2. **Time yourself.** Practice giving your presentation so you will know how much time your talk takes. Make it realistic. You need to do this practice run-through a couple of times so that you become comfortable with your material and your pacing. Timing your talk won't be helpful if you are racing through it or stumbling over sections during your presentation.

3. **Know what to add or delete.** Part of your preparation is antici-
pating time concerns, and knowing what material you can easily
add to or eliminate from your talk. To add extra material, have
additional research, statistics, or stories that highlight your key
points at the ready. The opposite approach is effective when you
need to shorten your remarks. Know ahead of time what material
is not crucial for reinforcing your key points, and don't discuss
those items. Speaking faster is not a substitute for the elimination
of material.

PRESCRIPTION FOR SUCCESS

Don't lose track of the time once you are in front of your audience. Arrange to have someone
close to the front give you an unobtrusive signal to alert you that you have only a certain
amount of time left.

35. Tips to Encourage Questions from Your Audience

How do I get people in my audience to ask questions?

A vice president of a major healthcare company asked me this question during one of our coaching sessions on presentation skills.

No one had ever asked me that before!

Often, presenters want to avoid anything to do with the Q&A segment of a presentation, but he wanted questions so he would know whether his audience had grasped his concepts. This desire for feedback is just one reason to encourage questions. There are others.

For example, you seem more approachable as a speaker when you take questions. Plus, how you answer the questions, and participate in any discussion that follows, can help explain or enhance your ideas and clarify any misunderstandings. In addition, the types of questions asked may let you know your participants' opinions of your suggestions.

Try these suggestions to encourage people to ask questions:

1. **Let the audience know when you will be taking questions.** Don't assume your audience members know that there will be a Q&A segment; tell them at the beginning of your talk. In a more informal talk or training session, participants may be encouraged to ask questions throughout. ("I'm open for questions throughout my presentation.") Or if the presenter doesn't want to interrupt the flow, he or she can ask the audience to wait to ask questions. ("Please save your questions until the end of my talk.")

2. **Nonverbally encourage questions.** Keep your body language open and don't cross your arms. Look at your audience. Move toward audience members when you can. Pause after you ask for questions—don't rush to start talking. This gives the participants a few seconds to formulate their ideas.

3. **Use an open-ended question.** If you say to your audience, "What questions do you have?" you are telling participants you assume that they have questions, and as a result, they're more likely to speak up. It is easy for people to say no if you simply ask, "Do you have any questions?"

4. **Request questions on a specific topic.** You can expand on the open-ended question by pinpointing a particular area of your presentation. For example, if you have discussed the budget, you can ask, "What questions do you have about the new budget items?" Also, asking about something you just discussed can help you transition from one part of your talk to another.

5. **Have participants write their questions and submit them before-hand.** This can be effective with large audiences or audiences at remote locations, when the questions can relate to your topic but are not dependent on the content of your presentation. You can answer some of the questions during your presentation, or refer to them at the end.

PRESCRIPTION FOR SUCCESS

Be prepared with your own first question. If you ask for questions and no one speaks up, you can offer one of your own by saying, "A question I am often asked is . . . ." Hearing you answer a question often makes audience members feel more comfortable asking their own questions. Or you might consider coordinating with a participant before your presentation, and arrange for that person to get things started by asking a specific question.

36. Answer Questions Like a Pro

I won't give a presentation because I'm petrified at the thought of answering questions.

I don't like giving presentations, but I really dislike the Q&A session.

I never know what to say when I'm asked a question, and I end up rambling.

Many people fear giving presentations. Yet as the three quotes above illustrate, there are people in my seminars who dislike the Q&A part of a presentation even more. They seem to dread losing control of the presentation or being caught off guard.

Answering questions effectively in front of your audience builds your credibility. Mastering the following points will help you appear poised and confident during the Q&A:

1. **Prepare for questions.** As you prepare your presentation, you also need to prepare for the questions you may be asked. Think about your topic and who is in your audience, and consider what they are likely to ask. Expect the questions, and know how you will answer them.

2. **Anticipate the tough questions.** Think about what difficult, annoying, or nasty questions you may be asked, and know how you will respond. Don't just pray that someone won't ask that question. Know how you will answer it.

3. **Repeat each question before answering.** This is hard to remember to do, but very important. You repeat the question for a number of reasons. When you repeat a question, it allows everyone to hear what was asked. You also gain a couple of seconds to get your thoughts together. And if the question is a hostile one, you

can paraphrase it and eliminate the hostility. For example, if the question is, "How come you are spending so much money on transportation?" you could paraphrase and say something like, "The question concerns the transportation budget."

4. **Don't be a puppet on your audience's string.** Resist the "feeding-frenzy" mentality if many audience members start shouting questions at once. Choose a question and then repeat it before answering. If you don't, you are being controlled by the audience as you try to answer one question after another. When you take the time to repeat the question, you gain control of the Q&A, as you are deciding which questions to address, and in what order.

5. **Look at the audience when answering the question.** When you repeat the question, look at the person who asked it. But when you answer the question, look at the audience to include everyone in the answer.

6. **Don't know the answer? Admit it.** Even when you are well prepared, there still may be times you are asked a question to which you don't know the answer. When that happens, you can usually say, "I don't know, but I will find out and get back to you." And make sure you do.

7. **Give your best educated guess.** Occasionally, there may be times when you don't know the answer, but you have to respond. You can then give what I call your best educated guess. This is not lying. It's a general response without being specific. It is saying something like, "Based on my experience (or research, or knowledge of . . .), I assume the following would occur: . . . ." (But make sure it is your best educated guess—don't go beyond the boundaries of what is plausible.)

8. **Defer answering, if the answer to the question will be explained later in your talk.** Often, you can say, "I am going to hold off answering that question as I will be discussing that topic in a few minutes." Of course, if the CEO asks the question, you may want to answer it right away!

9. **Don't end abruptly.** When the Q&A segment is nearing its end, prepare the audience. You can say something like, "I have time for one more question." And after you answer that question, move on to your closing.

PRESCRIPTION FOR SUCCESS

After you have answered someone's question, do not ask, "Did that answer your question?" You could be setting yourself up, as the person may respond, "No." And then what do you do? If the questioner wants more information, he or she will let you know — or seek you out later.

37. Show-and-Tell: Suggestions for Using Slides Successfully

If I hear one more speaker say, "I know you can't read this slide, but . . . ," I will scream. My time is being wasted.

Slides are intended to enhance your business presentation. They should supplement and support your talk, but not be the talk. They can help you to organize your thoughts and make it easier for the audience to understand your comments.

There are several presentation software options available, including PowerPoint, Keynote, Google Slides, and Prezi. Yet many people use slides incorrectly, as the saying "death by PowerPoint" implies. You don't want to bore the people in your audience or overwhelm them. Here are some general suggestions for using slides successfully.

- **Talk to the audience, not the screen.** The audience does not want to see your back as you discuss a slide. Also, position yourself so you do not block the screen.

- **Know how to use the equipment.** Practice your talk using your slides. Use a presentation remote control to advance them. Make the screen go to black if you have finished with one slide but will not be discussing the next slide right away. This forces the audience to focus on you. Most remote controls have a button for this. If your remote doesn't, try pressing "B." On most keyboards, it will switch the screen to black.

- **Use a title slide with your name on it.** Include more information, such as your job title or company, when speaking to people who do not know you.

- **Make your slides visually appealing.** Use an easily read font (Arial, Calibri, and Verdana are three good choices) and make it large enough for people to be able to read your comments—usually 28-point type or larger. Don't overload your slides with a lot of text. If you say, "I know you can't read this, but . . . ," the audience is thinking, "Then why are you showing it to me!" Add some color, but don't go overboard with exceptionally bright colors. Prezi has pan and zoom effects. Do not overwhelm your audience with these options, either.

- **Include a photograph or graphic that conveys your point.** These images make your slides more interesting. There are stock photo sites on the web, some of which charge a fee and some that have free images, or you can use your own photographs (if they are of good quality). If you work for a larger company, check with your art or graphics department—it may have images you can use.

- **Be smart if using a list of bullet points.** Each point should be just the key words, not whole thoughts. You will fill in the blanks and explain the complete concept in your talk. This helps underscore your credibility in front of your audience. Use a "build" to control what your audience sees. Do this by revealing only one bullet point at a time. After you finish discussing that point, reveal the next bullet point. If you show all the bullet points at once, the audience will be reading your points, not listening to you.

Exercise

Spend some time experimenting with different presentation options. Many companies have classes on using these tools. There are also online tutorials available. The more comfortable you become with slides, the better your presentations will be.

PRESCRIPTION FOR SUCCESS

Remember that slides are only part of your presentation. Even if you have the best slides available, they will not save a poor delivery by the speaker.

38. I'm Speaking on a Panel: What Do I Do?

I agreed to speak on a panel, thinking it would be easier than giving a talk by myself. But I am having second thoughts.

My boss signed me up to speak on a panel. Help! What do I do now?

Many professionals have experienced sentiments similar to these. At some point in your career, you may be asked or assigned to be on a panel. I encourage you to think of the task as a compliment, since presenting on a panel can help build your reputation.

When you are scheduled to be on a panel, keep this in mind: It's the moderator's job to keep things running smoothly during the panel discussion. It is your job to be ready to present.

Many of the points already discussed in this section are also useful for putting together a panel presentation. In addition, consider these items:

1. **Be familiar with the other panel members.** Look them up on LinkedIn, or ask your network. The moderator of the panel also may send you their bios. What are the panelists' areas of expertise? Do they have strong opinions about specific topics? You want to know what they are likely to say.

2. **Know the agenda.** What is the key focus of the panel? When will you speak? How much time do you have? Are you speaking on a specific topic, or will you be answering preassigned questions? The moderator should provide this information.

3. **Prepare.** Organize your comments, be concise, and keep to your allotted time. Also, phrase your comments so that they are easily understood by your listeners. The other panel members may be

experts, but your audience may not be. Include stories to help people remember what you said (See Chapter 26 for more information on stories.)

4. **Pay attention to your delivery.** Speak up and speak clearly. Make sure you are close enough to the mic to be heard. Look at the audience when you speak, not at the moderator or the other panelists.

5. **Interact with the other panelists . . . to a point.** Reference other people's comments, and build upon them when you can. Don't interrupt other panelists, and don't get into any heated arguments. A little disagreement can be interesting, but don't get carried away. You can agree to disagree.

6. **Look interested when others are speaking.** Even if you find the other panelists boring, don't show it on your face. Remember the social media stir prompted by the deer-in-the-headlights look on New Jersey Governor Chris Christie's face when he stood behind Donald Trump at a press conference during the 2016 primary elections? Be aware of how you will appear to the audience. Also, do not check your phone or text when others are speaking.

7. **Participate in the Q&A.** Often, at the end of a panel discussion, the moderator will solicit questions from the audience. If the moderator doesn't ask a specific panelist to answer each question, make sure you respond to some of them. You also can add on to someone else's response.

PRESCRIPTION FOR SUCCESS

Stay around after your session. It's a way to have more interaction with your audience members. Many of them likely will have more questions. This is also the time when people may ask for your business card, so make sure you bring a supply to your session. And don't forget to ask for other people's business cards too.

39. Polish Your Presentations a Little More

After my presentation a colleague told me that I looked up at the ceiling a lot, as if seeking divine inspiration! I had no idea I had this habit.

Even when we think we have a presentation just the way we want it, we may discover something that needs improvement. This entire segment of the book has focused on helping you to prepare and deliver successful presentations. But we are not done quite yet. There are still a few more tips to help you shine when you're in front of an audience.

Some of the essential points have been stressed already. They include ways to prepare and practice your speech. Never underestimate the importance of preparation. As Mark Twain said: "It usually takes me more than three weeks to prepare a good impromptu speech."

As also discussed, it's important to make presentations often and to review any you were able to record. As the example of the New Jersey governor in Chapter 38 illustrates, how you think you appear when you are in front of an audience may be very different from the reality that the audience sees and hears.

Additional ways to enhance your speaking skills include:

1. **Take a presentation skills class.** Many companies provide these seminars as part of their training curriculum. Sign up if you are eligible to attend. Some colleges also offer such classes as part of their continuing education offerings.

2. **Observe other speakers in your company.** Were their presentations effective? Why? What did you notice about their body language, voice, and so on? Learn from your observations, but keep your comments to yourself. Do not give unsolicited critical feedback to the speaker! You can, of course, tell a speaker that he or she did a good job.

3. **Watch TED Talks.** You can watch interesting talks delivered by experts in their fields by going to ted.com, a "platform for ideas worth spreading." This was originally a site with presentations on technology, entertainment, and design (which is what TED stands for). Now there are thousands of talks available on numerous topics. Learn from these talks and evaluate the speakers' delivery.

4. **Familiarize yourself with business-oriented websites.** These include BusinessInsider.com, Forbes.com, and Entrepreneur.com, which often provide helpful articles.

5. **Hire a coach.** There are numerous coaches who can help fine-tune your skills. I have often coached senior executives who sought specific help as they prepared for a special presentation before their board of directors or their employees.

6. **Join Toastmasters.** Toastmasters is an organization with chapters around the world. Members attend meetings, learn about presentation skills, listen to other speakers, make presentations, and gain feedback.

7. **Use the Post-Presentation Checklist.** Review the next chapter and use the checklist to analyze your own presentations.

PRESCRIPTION FOR SUCCESS

Evaluate your feedback. Often, colleagues and bosses will comment on your presentation — but not all feedback is useful. If your boss tells you, "You need to do a better job," it is difficult to learn anything from that statement. You may be able to respond, "Thanks for the feedback. What exactly can I do to improve?" This might elicit more specific information, such as "You need to speak more slowly."

40. Continue to Improve: Use the Post-Presentation Checklist to Evaluate

Review this checklist after you make a presentation and note areas that need improvement. Consider the solutions under the boxes you checked. Work on those areas as you prepare for your next presentation.

❏ I had **stage fright.**

- Say positive things to myself before my next presentation
- Practice out loud
- Remind myself that the audience doesn't know I'm nervous unless I tell or show them

❏ My **introduction** was not effective.

- I need an attention statement
- My objective needs to be stated clearly
- I should provide more information when I introduce myself

❏ I need to use more **stories** to illustrate my points.

- Develop my story file

❏ My **posture, eye contact, and/or gestures** were distractions.

- Review any recordings of my presentation to identify problems areas

❏ I need to **dress** more professionally for the audience.

- Observe what the higher-ups wear when they give presentations

❑ My use of **filler words** conveyed to the audience that I was nervous or not prepared.

- Review any recordings of my talk to identify filler words
- Monitor my everyday speech for filler words, and strive to eliminate them

❑ I was not comfortable answering **questions**.

- Review the questions asked by the audience and formulate answers for the future
- Anticipate tough questions and prepare my answers

❑ Other items to consider:

- Did I project my **voice**?
- Did my **transitions** connect my points?
- Did I talk to my **slides** instead of to the audience?
- Did my **conclusion** need a summary and/or a memorable statement?

PART III

TALK ISN'T CHEAP: ASSERTIVE COMMUNICATION AND CONFLICT

There are lots of colloquial sayings about communication.

You probably have heard the expression, "If you don't have anything nice to say, don't say anything at all." Unfortunately, that expression can encourage passive behavior.

You may have also heard the saying that advocates a different attitude: "Don't get mad, get even!" And unfortunately, this can promote nasty, aggressive behavior.

But there is an alternative approach: assertive behavior. I have a saying for this: "Say what you want to say, need to say, and choose to say in a polite and powerful manner."

This "polite and powerful" attitude allows you to express yourself during day-to-day interactions, difficult conversations, and confrontational situations in ways that will make you feel good about yourself, help you to build positive relationships, enhance your professional reputation, and often get you what you want.

If you are only polite in today's society, people may see you as meek and a pushover. If you are just powerful, you can come across as aggressive. It is the combination of the two that I believe will make you truly successful when communicating in today's business world.

Why wouldn't you try such a winning approach?

41. Are You Too Nice?
Learn the "Three Faces of Communication"

Can you be too nice when communicating with others?

A woman in one of my seminars asked if it was possible for her to be "too nice" when interacting with her coworkers, customers, or bosses. She told me that she often felt invisible around them.

My answer was simple,: "Yes, you can be too nice . . . and passive." Let me explain.

A few years ago I created the Three Faces of Communication model (see figure) to help people understand whether they were passive, aggressive, or assertive when interacting with others. This continuum, along with information in the next chapter, will help you identify where you fall along the spectrum of too nice (passive), polite and powerful (assertive), or the tough one (aggressive).

Three Faces of Communication model

Too Nice	Polite and Powerful	The Tough One

As you review the following descriptions, you probably won't identify with all of the characteristics of any one style, but you most likely have more attributes of one style than another.

Too Nice/Passive

If you are too nice, you often exhibit passive behavior. You put other people before yourself and ignore your own thoughts, feelings, and beliefs. You have a difficult time voicing your opinion. But you do complain to others. Since you don't want to hurt people's feelings, you find it difficult to confront them about your concerns. You are overly friendly with colleagues or employees, and they sometimes take advantage of your kind nature. You have a difficult time saying no, and overburden yourself as a result.

The Tough One/Aggressive

If you are the tough one, you usually exhibit aggressive behavior. You only consider your own thoughts, feelings, and beliefs and ignore everyone else's. You want your way and can be a bully about getting it. You can yell, insult, berate, curse, have a harsh tone, and put people down. When you confront someone, you believe that "the jerk had it coming." You can be difficult to work with, and problems can go unresolved because your colleagues or employees steer clear of you.

Polite and Powerful/Assertive

If you are polite and powerful, you exhibit assertive behavior. You take not only your own thoughts, feelings, and beliefs into account, but those of others, too. You are polite to people, and you will speak up clearly, calmly, and directly. You voice your opinions about things that bother you, and you know how to manage conflict and get problems resolved. You don't curse or yell. You are fair and up front with people.

Once you have a sense of your communication style, the goal would be to remain in or move toward the polite and powerful (assertive) middle. The next chapter starts the discussion of what specific assertive behaviors look like.

PRESCRIPTION FOR SUCCESS

There may be times when you choose to move more toward the passive or aggressive ends of this continuum. That's understandable, as few people stay on an even keel all the time. The key is to be aware of your behavior and its ramifications.

42. How Assertive Are You?
Take a Self-Assessment

I thought I was assertive, but I guess I wasn't. My comments were ignored.

One of the first steps in becoming an assertive person is being aware of your current behavior. The previous chapter provided general descriptions of passive, assertive, and aggressive communication. It is time to start looking at the specifics—how you speak, act, and behave with others. As the quote above implies (and I have heard variations of this comment from many people), we are not always aware of what makes up assertive behavior.

Below is a self-assessment. Please think carefully about each of the comments, decide whether it reflects your behavior, and respond *yes*, *no*, or *unsure* to each one. Your answers will provide important information about how you present yourself in the workplace.

	Yes	No	Unsure
1. I freely offer my opinion at meetings.	❑	❑	❑
2. I eliminate discounting words from my comments, such as *actually*, *kind of*, or *just*.	❑	❑	❑
3. I speak loudly enough for others to hear me.	❑	❑	❑
4. I tell other people when their behavior creates a problem for me.	❑	❑	❑
5. I can say no to others without feeling guilty.	❑	❑	❑
6. I look people in the eye when communicating with them.	❑	❑	❑
7. My gestures are assertive, not aggressive— I don't point or pound on furniture.	❑	❑	❑

	Yes	No	Unsure
8. I make sure not to play with my hands, rings, or rubber bands when speaking to others.	❏	❏	❏
9. I can express myself to others clearly and concisely, without yelling or cursing.	❏	❏	❏
10. I maintain a pleasant facial expression and don't smile or frown inappropriately.	❏	❏	❏

These 10 statements describe key assertive behaviors. Ideally, you answered *yes* to all of them. If you did, congratulations; you believe you are assertive. But before you start celebrating, *remember that this self-assessment is your impression of you. Others may see you differently.* You need to know if such a gap in perception exists. Make sure you read through the rest of this section with a critical eye, evaluating honestly whether you really are exhibiting these behaviors.

If you answered *no* or *unsure* to any of these comments, pay special attention to those areas when you read about them in this section. Demonstrating the behaviors listed is key to having an assertive presence.

Exercise

Periodically review the self-assessment. Have your answers changed? Are you moving toward the polite and powerful middle? Choose just one or two items to concentrate on at a time. It will help you monitor your behavior.

PRESCRIPTION FOR SUCCESS

Identify an assertive role model in your company, community, or professional organization. Observe the person's actions. What's working for that person? Which of these behaviors do you want to imitate? You can learn a lot from watching others with a keen eye. As Confucius said, "If I am walking with two other men, each of them will serve as my teacher. I will pick out the good points of one and imitate them, and the bad points of the other and correct them in myself."

43. Should I Believe You?
Avoid Sending Mixed Messages

I didn't trust him. He said he was open to my comments, but he was frowning and crossed his arms as I spoke.

As the above comment indicates, your words can send one message, but your body language and voice can send another. You communicate with others both verbally and nonverbally.

And research has shown that people will believe your nonverbal communication before they believe your words.

To be assertive, you want to be consistent, which means that your verbal and nonverbal communication should send the same message. The self-assessment in Chapter 42 highlighted many of the assertive—that is, polite and powerful—ways to communicate. Here are some considerations to help prevent sending mixed messages.

1. **Don't let your body contradict you.** When standing, do not slouch, cross your ankles, or play with your hands. These behaviors will make you appear passive, regardless of how strongly you believe in your comments. Do not point your finger at someone or pound on the table when talking. You will appear aggressive, regardless of your words. To point assertively, use an open palm and keep your fingers together.

2. **Don't look away.** In the United States, if you look away, or mostly look away, when speaking, people may perceive you—and what you are saying—as not to be trusted.

3. **Control your voice.** Many people speak softly. If people can't hear you, your words won't register and you will appear passive. If you speak too loudly, and a few people do, you will appear aggressive.

4. **Be aware of your facial expression.** If you are smiling when discussing bad news, would people believe that you are upset? Probably not. The same is true if you are discussing good news and you're frowning. As mentioned in the section on presentation skills (Chapter 28), you want your facial expression to be consistent with your words.

5. **Avoid sarcasm.** You will appear to be mocking other people if your words are sarcastic and deliberately say the opposite of what you mean. And it could backfire on you. To use a fictional illustration, an episode of the television show *Major Crimes* featured police officers who were eager to open the trunk of a murder suspect's car, but they didn't have a search warrant. Sarcastically, the smart-mouth suspect said, "Jimmy Hoffa [the long-missing former Teamsters leader] is in my trunk." His taunting comment created probable cause. The police chief responded, "Take him at his word," and the officers opened the trunk and found the evidence they had originally sought. You may not have to deal with murder suspects, but the likelihood of sarcasm backfiring is the same.

QUESTION TO CONSIDER

Q. *I often say "I think" when voicing my opinions. Am I sending mixed messages?*

A. Possibly. People often say "I think" when they actually know. As a result, they come across as tentative. If you say, "I think the project will be finished on time," you are saying you are unsure. But if you know, be clear about it, and state: "The project will be finished on time."

PRESCRIPTION FOR SUCCESS

Watch your language. Avoid sentences with weak beginnings. Wishy-washy phrases or disclaimers undermine the content of any statement. These include comments such as "I may be wrong about this . . ." or "I am not sure . . ." or "This is probably a stupid suggestion, but . . . ."

44. Eliminate the Negativity—No Harsh, Aggressive Tones

A colleague told me that during one of her training sessions, while she was explaining a number of ways to overcome writer's block, a participant interrupted and said, "You failed to mention one of the important ones." She said she wanted to throw a book at him—even though he was correct and she did forget to mention one item on her list.

This colleague was not upset because of what the participant said, but because of how he expressed himself. As German philosopher Friedrich Nietzsche observed: "We often dispute an opinion when what we really object to is the tone in which the opinion is offered."

A harsh tone can be conveyed in a number of ways—including a speaker's choice of words. It is easy to feel attacked if you are interacting with people who express themselves negatively. The participant in my colleague's seminar used the wording, "You failed . . . ," and as a result, his comment became a harsh, blaming statement.

People don't like to be blamed. When they are, it's easy for them to respond aggressively, as evidenced by my colleague's desire to throw a book. The participant could have expressed the same information in a neutral way, by saying, "There is one more item to be added to your list."

If you eliminate the negativity in your comments, you have a better chance of making a positive impression. I am not suggesting that you can't express difficult thoughts or strong feelings, or even say no when necessary. But often the same sentiments can be expressed assertively—without using off-putting language.

Consider these three suggestions:

1. **Replace negative words with positive or neutral ones, when possible.** As discussed in Part I on written communication, avoid using negative words in conversation. In these examples, which would you rather hear?

   - "That's a stupid idea" (negative). Or "We are not able to support this idea because . . ." (neutral).

   - "I don't want my people viewed as unprofessional or incompetent" (negative). Or "I want my people viewed as professional and competent" (positive).

2. **Avoid using a negative verb after the pronoun *you*.** These "you" statements often come across as blaming, aggressive comments. For instance:

   - "You missed the deadline." Rephrase this: "The deadline has passed."

   - "You failed to include the latest numbers in your presentation." Instead, say something like: "Remember to include the latest numbers in your presentation."

   Sometimes, replacing the "you" phrasing with an "I" statement can eliminate the negativity. You are no longer blaming someone when you use an "I" message, but taking ownership of your comments. Do you hear the difference between the following comments?

   - "You're wrong." Or "I see it differently."

   - "You are not explaining it correctly." Or "I'm not understanding what you are saying."

3. **Say no to someone's request without sounding harsh.** The secret is to mention, when possible, what you *can* do. Often, you don't need to say the word *no*. This type of wording also can help you refrain from agreeing to things that you don't want to do—without feeling guilty. For example:

- A colleague wants to meet you at an inconvenient time. You can say, "I am unable to meet you then. I am available after . . . ."

- A customer wants you to do something, but you are not able to meet the requirements. You can say, "I am not able to because . . . . Here's what I can do for you."

PRESCRIPTION FOR SUCCESS

Correct people only when necessary. If someone said the program began in 2013, but it really was 2014, do you need to point that out? And do you need to do so publicly? If the difference is not significant, you may appear as someone who nitpicks, or who likes to make others look bad.

45. Avoid the Use of the Word *But*, but . . .

I knew that bad news was coming as soon as I heard the word but.

We discuss the use of the word *but* in my assertiveness classes. One seminar participant, who made the comment above, then added: "Amazing that one little word could have such an impact."

For many people, *but* can be a red flag. When they hear the word, they stop listening. For example, if a boss says to someone, "You did a nice job, but . . . ," the employee knows that what follows won't be complimentary.

Generally, *but* negates any positive comments that come before it.

One woman told me that *but* should stand for "behold the underlying truth." And usually that is true! It's generally more effective to use the word *and*. "You did a nice job, *and* it would be even more effective if . . . ." People also use *however* or *though* as a substitute for *but*. These can work, but my preference is still the use of *and*.

During a discussion in one of my classes, a sales representative jumped in and excitedly asked, "But, but, but, aren't there times you *want* to use *but*?" After the class stopped laughing, I responded that she was right. There are times you may choose to use *but*, especially if you want to contradict something—which she had just done.

When the comments before the *but* are negative, off-putting, or pessimistic, the *but* can negate them, too—or at least soften the impact. An example of that might be: "We didn't make our quota for the first quarter, but we are hopeful for a better result in the second quarter."

PRESCRIPTION FOR SUCCESS

Pay attention to your use of what I call contradictory phrases. These occur when you say no as the first part of a response, but follow it with wording that seems contradictory. For example, you might agree with someone by saying, "No, I agree." It also pops up when you tell someone that he or she is correct by saying, "No, you're right." Other examples include, "No, I'm certain," "No, you're fine," and "No, I'm sure." Many people may not notice this verbal idiosyncrasy immediately—but once they become aware of its use by others, it can drive them crazy. The solution: Simply drop the "No," or replace it with a positive, as in "Yes, you're right."

46. Do You Have a Problem with "No Problem"?

Should I respond with "You're welcome" or "No problem" when someone thanks me?

A number of participants in my assertiveness and etiquette seminars have asked this question, or a version of it.

I usually respond by explaining that although we work in a relatively informal business environment, and although our language is constantly evolving, the responses "You're welcome" and "No problem" are not interchangeable. They mean different things.

"You're welcome" is the shortened form for "You are welcome to it"—meaning you are welcome to my help, my gift, my advice, and the like.

People want you to take their expressions of appreciation seriously. If someone says, "Thanks for the birthday gift" or "Thank you for all your hard work; it really helped us out," the appropriate response is "You're welcome." You are acknowledging the other person's thanks in a polite way.

"No problem" is the shortened form for "That is not a problem for me," and it can sound glib if offered as a response to "Thank you."

If a colleague emails you that he has had to change the location for your meeting, your response may be "No problem." You are acknowledging that what someone said or did in a particular situation is not causing difficulty for you.

People tend to have strong opinions on this topic.

During the research on this subject, I came across an article by Bill Flanagan, a contributor to the television show *Sunday Morning*. He expressed his frustration that young people will say "No problem" in response to almost any situation. He used the example of his employee who, when repeatedly confronted about arriving late to work, and told to be on time in the future, would respond, "No problem." Yet the young man continued to arrive late and was eventually let go.

So, is this all-purpose use of "No problem" a generational difference? Time will tell—remember what we said above about language constantly evolving. Some online sites, including a couple of informal dictionary sites, seem to disregard the differences in nuance and interpretation between the two responses. But in the business world, clarity and good manners should always prevail over the use of imprecise slang expressions.

PRESCRIPTION FOR SUCCESS

Whether you say "You're welcome" or "No problem," you have to say something. Not responding or saying "Uh-huh" when someone thanks you is not okay!

47. Listen Up! You Can't Talk and Pay Attention at the Same Time

Let me put my glasses on so I can hear you.

When a seminar participant said this to me, I thought she had a hearing aid on her glasses. She didn't. She said that in order to focus on what someone was saying, she needed to see the person.

As an assertive person, you, too, need to concentrate on the other person. I love the saying, "You were given two ears and one mouth for a reason. You need to listen more than you speak." Here are eight suggestions to make you a better listener:

1. **Get ready to listen.** To the degree that you can, get into a quiet, nondistracting setting. Close the door, if there is one. As one young man from a social media company told me, "We have an open, noisy office. When I really need to listen, I will meet with people in our small conference room." Turn away from your computer and look the person in the eye.

2. **Let the other person talk!** For some of us, this is the hardest task of all. Don't interrupt the person. Also, it's rude to finish sentences for other people.

3. **Do not immediately start problem-solving.** Many times, people are not looking for solutions; they just need to talk. You may be solving a problem that doesn't exist or preventing people from coming up with their own solutions.

4. **Be aware of your filters.** We are very quick to make judgments about others, and then, based upon those judgments, we either listen or don't listen to them. Imagine your doorman gave you a stock tip: Would you value that opinion? Many would answer no, making a judgment based on what that person does for a living.

Yet it is very possible that your doorman knows what he is talking about. Listen to people so you can evaluate whether they are knowledgeable about their topics.

5. **Use verbal prompts.** These are words like *okay*, *I see*, *yes*, and *uh-hum*. They are not filler words. Used occasionally, they let the speaker know that you are listening, and they're especially important when you are listening to someone on the phone. If you don't use verbal prompts, the person is likely to say, "Are you there?"

6. **Ask good questions or make comments.** You often need more information to make sure you fully understand a situation, or to get the complete story. Ask questions like, "What else happened?" or "What do you think?" to elicit additional information. Or simply say, "Tell me more" to get the person talking.

7. **Put away your phone.** As mentioned throughout this book, the presence of a phone inhibits conversation. You want to give the other person your undivided attention.

8. **Use your own words.** You can paraphrase someone's comments to indicate understanding. This is when you repeat in your own words what you thought the speaker said. Using phrases like, "If I understand correctly, you're saying . . . ," "You're implying that . . . ," or "Let me get this right. You think . . ." lets the person know that you have heard him or her.

PRESCRIPTION FOR SUCCESS

Create a signal to remind yourself to listen. Years ago, I put a small sign with the letters "KYMS" at the back of my desk (where only I could see it). It stood for "Keep your mouth shut." It was a very helpful reminder to listen, especially when I was on the phone.

48. Silence Isn't Always Golden: Voice Your Opinion at Meetings

In a "Corner Office" column in the New York Times, *Sharon Napier, CEO of Partners + Napier, stressed the importance of voicing your opinion when she said: "Don't sit quietly and think about things and maybe whisper to somebody or tell people afterward. Put yourself out there, and get involved in the conversation."*

Many people are reluctant to speak up at meetings but regret later that they didn't have any input. Check your behavior against this list of assertiveness points to make sure your voice is heard.

1. **Be ready.** Think about the meeting, who is going to be there, and what may be discussed. If there is an agenda, review it in advance. Consider the possible topics, and know what you want to say about them. By doing this, you will be able to express your comments with confidence when and if the topic comes up.

2. **Establish your presence.** Walk into the room as though you belong there. Greet people. If you feel comfortable being in the room, you will feel more confident about saying something at the meeting. When you sit down, make sure to say hello to the people on either side of you.

3. **Understand the consequences of staying quiet.** If you don't speak up, your bosses, colleagues, and customers won't know what you know, and you can be overlooked and discounted as irrelevant. Jenny Ming, chief executive of the clothing chain Charlotte Russe, was also quoted in the *New York Times'* "Corner Office" column cited above. She said: "What I learned is that you can't assume that people know what you're thinking or what you want in your career. You have to speak up."

4. **Speak early.** The longer you wait to offer your opinion, the harder it becomes to speak and the more invisible you become. Find some credible reason to make a comment or ask a question near the beginning of a meeting. When you speak, stand if it is appropriate—this ensures the meeting participants will have to look up at you.

5. **Don't ask permission to speak.** You are a valid participant in the meeting. You don't need others' consent to talk. Say, "I have a comment," or simply provide your opinion.

6. **Interrupt when needed.** Know the protocols of your meetings. Usually, interrupting is an annoying speaking habit, but in some instances it is necessary if you are to have your opinion heard. (See Chapter 52 for more on interruptions.)

PRESCRIPTION FOR SUCCESS

Be careful not to overtalk in a meeting. People will tune you out or avoid you if you do. Examples of overtalking include:

- Giving too many facts or details about the topic
- Going off on tangents, providing information that is irrelevant
- Repeating the same thing over and over

Make sure your comments are pertinent, and express them succinctly.

49. What's My Line? What to Say in Awkward Situations

A younger colleague told me I am pretty savvy about social media "for an old guy." I think he meant it as a compliment, but I'm only about 15 years older than he is. How do I respond without sounding rude?

Many people have difficulty figuring out what to say in uncomfortable or annoying circumstances, as this comment from a (still fairly young) man brings up.

To learn to handle life's bothersome situations, you need an assertive strategy such as my *What's My Line* response. The "line" is a comment that is both polite and powerful. You plan your line ahead of time so that you know what to say when you encounter an awkward situation. If you are uncomfortable about speaking up, having a prepared line makes it easier to do so.

Here are some difficult situations that often arise, and some lines you can use to deal with them effectively. These examples may not fit your situation exactly, but you can adapt them and use them for inspiration.

- **Someone cuts in front of you in line.** Don't assume the person is a jerk. It is possible he or she did not realize that you were there, or was preoccupied and not paying attention.

  Your polite and powerful line: "I believe I was here first."

- **Someone yells or screams at you.** People can lose their cool sometimes and start screaming. Some may not realize they are yelling. If you speak up assertively, they may calm down. (If you are concerned for your safety, however, contact security.)

  Your polite and powerful line: "I want to help, but screaming at me won't help me help you. It will only make us both unproductive." Or "I want to talk about this, but not this way." You may need to raise your volume a little so the other person hears you.

- **Someone gives you a compliment.** Many people are uncomfortable when given a compliment. One director said that when he compliments his administrative assistant on her excellent work, her response is often something like, "It was no big deal."

   Your polite and powerful line: "Thank you." Or "Thank you. I appreciate that." Then stop talking.

- **Someone calls you by the wrong name.** You need to correct the person. If not, he or she will keep calling you by the wrong name. The longer you leave this kind of situation uncorrected, the more difficult it becomes to address the situation.

   Your simple, polite and powerful line: "My name is . . . ."

- **Someone makes a thoughtless comment.** You may be uncomfortable with the comment, but it's not necessarily offensive. People often speak before they realize that their words can bother others. The "for an old guy" comment mentioned above fits into this category. You can let it go, or you can say something.

   This man's polite and powerful line was: "Of course I'm savvy. I've been on Facebook since its birth." This response was lighthearted, and certainly was better than being rude. He also could have said a simple, "Thank you."

Exercise

Think about the awkward, difficult situations you encounter. Come up with a "polite and powerful" line to use. Try out your line when you can. Evaluate how it works. Should you continue to use it, or create a different one?

PRESCRIPTION FOR SUCCESS

Keep your line short and sweet. Do not give your life story. I have a broken blood vessel on my face, and people often come up to me and say that I have lipstick on my cheek. One client even tried to remove it. It can be awkward, so I needed a line. I could say, "I have been to a plastic surgeon and he can remove it, but he can't guarantee that it won't scar, and I don't want a scar. Plus, my mother said it was nicely placed on my face, so I'm keeping it." But I don't. My line is simply: "Thank you. It's permanent." People usually smile, or even laugh a little.

50. Two Communication Secrets to Get What You Want

A mother said to her three-year-old daughter: "When you get a chance, can you please clean your room?" The young girl responded: "Mom, no, I'm not gonna get a chance."

A client told me this story about her daughter, and after I stopped laughing, I had to tell her that she hadn't used a little-recognized, yet powerful communication tool. Since she had hired me to teach assertiveness for her organization, I felt comfortable giving her this feedback.

Her stumbling block?

My client had made her request using a question instead of a direct assertive statement. By asking ("Can you please clean your room?"), she gave the decision-making power to her daughter.

Using a direct statement, such as "Sweetie, I want you to clean your room before lunch," makes it very clear what you expect. Of course, there are no guarantees with three-year-olds, but even with children, you have a better chance of getting what you want when you are direct.

This secret also can work in the workplace. Listen to the difference: "Boss, I would like to be assigned to the ABC project" versus "Boss, can you assign me to the ABC project?" Both are polite, but one is slightly more likely to get the speaker what she wants. The direct statement—"Boss, I would like . . ."—usually has more success.

The second communication secret was summed up in *Star Wars: Episode V—The Empire Strikes Back*. In that movie, Yoda, the Jedi Master, proclaims: "Try not. Do, or do not. There is no try."

Be cautious with the use of the word *try* if you want others to be accountable for their action or inaction. If you say to your employee,

"Please try to keep to the schedule," he or she can always say later, "Well, I tried, but something else came up."

You can be polite and still use a straightforward statement, such as, "I need you to keep to the schedule."

To repeat: When you are direct, you are more likely to get what you want.

PRESCRIPTION FOR SUCCESS

Monitor yourself over the next few days. Is your word choice preventing you from getting what you want? If so, review the pointers above and make a conscious effort to rephrase your statements.

51. How to Manage "Know-It-Alls" Without Insult

There is one guy in my office who is driving me crazy. He is always offering his opinion about my work, and believes his way is the right way. What do I do? I want to respond, but I like him and don't want to offend him.

"Know-it-alls." There is one in every office.

Clearly, the man in my seminar who made the above comment was growing increasingly irritated by his colleague's unsolicited input. And when that happens, it can be tempting to say something like: "How do you know so much about things you know nothing about?"

But don't.

Though that line may be funny, it also may be considered insulting. I suggest trying the alternative approaches below, which let these opinionated people know that their comments are not the final word—but don't alienate them. You will speak up in a polite and powerful manner, and as a result, feel good that you responded. These approaches include:

1. Ask the person to explain his or her opinion by saying something like:

   - "What information (or facts or data) do you have to support that position?"
   - "How do you know that?" Or "How do you know that to be true?"

2. Acknowledge the difference in opinions by using lines like:

   - "I have a different viewpoint about it."
   - "I have a different opinion, and here's why."

- "My research/information supports a different position. Let's compare notes."

Regardless of the approach you choose, make sure you speak loudly enough to be heard, look the person in the eye, and do not have a negative tone in your voice.

Also recognize that either approach may lead to a discussion. Be open to considering other points of view. Sometimes even "know-it-alls" can be right or have a valid point.

PRESCRIPTION FOR SUCCESS

Do not say, "I'm sorry you feel that way." It's easy for the other person to respond, "No, you're not." And this is usually correct: You're not sorry.

52. "Hold That Thought!" and Other Ways to Handle Interruptions

What do you do when you are interrupted? I am getting so tired of people interrupting me. I want to scream.

Please, don't scream. If you do, you are being as rude as the person who interrupts. Yet I understand why people become annoyed when others interrupt them, as it means the original speaker's opinions, thoughts, or ideas are no longer being heard. Plus, when someone interrupts you, it can cause you to lose your train of thought or appear passive in front of others.

There is no one perfect way to handle interruptions, but there are several ways to try. Here are some of them:

1. **Hold your ground.** When someone interrupts you, you don't have to yield to that person. If you continue talking, with your volume slightly raised, the other person may realize that he or she interrupted you and stop talking.

2. **"Hold that thought."** You speak up assertively and say something like "Just a minute—I will get to that shortly." You also could put up your hand in a "wait" gesture when you speak up, but be careful that this gesture doesn't appear aggressive.

3. **Speak to the person.** In private, you can talk to your interrupter. You can say something like, "You have a tendency to interrupt me when I am giving my report. I lose my train of thought when you do that. I want to hear your comments; please wait until I'm finished talking before you offer them." Or use the shorter version, "Please wait until I'm finished talking before you add your comments."

4. **Let the person interrupt you.** If it is an infrequent occurrence, why not let it go. No one is perfect. You, too, may be guilty of being an interrupter at some point. Also, make sure that you are not talking too long, so that interrupting you is the only way other people can get a chance to say anything. You don't want to hog the conversation.

PRESCRIPTION FOR SUCCESS

Assuming you aren't monopolizing the meeting, don't make it easy for people to interrupt. If you speak slowly, people have lots of time to jump in between your words and take the floor from you. Record yourself. You may need to increase your speaking rate to discourage the interruptions. But don't overcorrect. Don't speak so quickly that people can't understand you.

53. Fightin' Words: Questions to Avoid Asking (or Answering) at Work

I can't believe he asked me whom I was going to vote for. We have a private ballot box for a reason!

It can be tempting to ask provocative, challenging, or personal questions. What's the harm in finding out whom your colleagues think should win the election, or asking their opinions about the death penalty?

Don't do it.

I know that asking questions is one of the ways to engage with people. Yet if you ask certain types of questions, you could embarrass people or get an answer you didn't expect or want. The discussion that follows can quickly escalate into an argument and easily become heated.

Avoid asking the following types of questions:

1. **Questions involving money.** These include anything along these lines:

   - "How can you afford that handbag?"
   - "How much money do you make?"
   - "What did you pay for your house?"

   The answers to questions like these are not your business, and by asking them, you are likely to make the other person uncomfortable.

2. **Political questions.** These include anything along these lines:

   - "Whom are you voting for?"
   - "How can you vote for . . . ?"

Your opinion of the person you're questioning can be altered, often negatively, if he or she is not voting for your candidate. And the other person's opinion of you may change, too.

3. **Questions on controversial topics.** These are similar to political questions. If you ask someone about his or her opinion on the death penalty, animal rights, abortion, and so on, you may get an answer you weren't expecting. You could subsequently get into an unpleasant exchange, as these are the kinds of topics on which people try to change others' beliefs.

4. **Very personal questions.** These include anything along these lines:

   - "What's your sexual orientation?"
   - "How old are you?"
   - "Are you pregnant?" (Avoid this one at all costs!)
   - "Are you having an affair with_____?"

   If your colleague wanted you to know the answers to these questions, he or she would have told you.

5. **Negative questions.** These include such questions as:

   - "How can you stand working with _____?"
   - "Don't you think the boss's position on _____ is outrageous?"
   - "Why did you cut your hair/shave your beard? I liked it better the other way."

   These questions are really judgment statements and can become fighting words.

PRESCRIPTION FOR SUCCESS

You don't have to answer every question asked of you. If you are asked one of the above questions, you can quickly excuse yourself from the conversation or change the topic. You also can be polite and powerful and tell the person, "I'm uncomfortable discussing this at work. Let's get back to business."

54. "How Can I Say This?"
Ways to Deliver Difficult News

I really didn't know how to have the conversation.

A vendor told a loyal customer that he would send her a job quote, but four weeks later she hadn't heard from him. The vendor finally texted her, "I've delayed telling you this, but I haven't done your quote because I'm too busy to do your work. Sorry. I really didn't know how to have this conversation."

She was furious with him. She said: "If he had told me right up front, I would have understood. But he caused me to waste a lot of time, and it set back my project. I won't use his services again."

How do you deliver difficult news? This type of situation is anxiety inducing, whether you have to admit to a client that you can't do her work, or you have to tell an employee he is about to be laid off. Here are five suggestions on how to convey an unwelcome message but still maintain a relationship with the recipient:

1. **Don't delay!** The longer you wait, the harder it gets. And the difficult situation won't disappear. Take a little time to get your thoughts together, but don't put off the discussion. When you do delay, you usually create more problems.

2. **Face up to your responsibility.** Don't delegate this assignment to someone else. If it is your job to deliver the news, you should do so.

3. **Choose the correct way.** It's usually best to talk face-to-face, but make sure you do so in a private setting where you won't be interrupted. Other people don't need to hear the discussion. If that is not possible, the telephone is the next best alternative. Email is informal, but it can work if most of your communication has been by email. Avoid sending difficult news via a text message. It is too impersonal and abrupt.

4. **Pick your words carefully.** Explain the situation without using aggressive language. Be honest without being cruel. Before you initiate a discussion, write down what you want to say. Read the words out loud. If the message sounds harsh to you, it will sound harsh to the other person.

5. **Offer alternatives, if you have them.** Saying "I'm unable to do this because . . . , but I can do this for you" will make the news easier for others to hear. A boss told his employee that she didn't get the promotion she'd been seeking, but added that he would help her find a training class to gain the necessary skills to move ahead.

QUESTION TO CONSIDER

Q. *My colleague had lipstick on her front teeth. Should I have said something?*

A. Yes. You can simply describe the situation, "Jen, you have lipstick on your teeth." Or "Tom, your fly is undone." Most people appreciate being saved from further embarrassment. If you are uncomfortable because of gender, get someone else to do it.

PRESCRIPTION FOR SUCCESS

Learn to express sympathy. The loss of a loved one is a difficult time for people, and expressing sympathy can be comforting to them. You can say, "I'm sorry for your loss." Or "I just heard the news and I'm sorry for your loss." Or "I'm sorry for your loss. I know how close you were to your grandmother." Offer to help, if appropriate: "Don't worry about the presentation. I will do your part for you."

55. No Pouting: Polite Ways to Handle Criticism

I can't get better without feedback. Let me have it!

One young man expressed this sentiment during one of my presentation skills seminars. As the class progressed, I, along with the other participants in the class, gave him many suggestions to enhance the delivery of his talk. And by the end of the training, his skills really improved!

As you advance in your career, you are bound to get feedback on your work. No doubt you will hear a lot of positive comments, but you also are likely to hear negative ones. How you receive this feedback is important to your career.

Follow these steps to learn how to handle criticism assertively and grow from the experience:

1. **Be open to the other person's comments.** Some of the feedback you receive may be difficult to hear, but don't get defensive. Do not cross your arms, as you immediately look closed off if you do. Keep your facial expression neutral; do not frown or pout. Make sure you look at the person. It is easy to dismiss the person criticizing your work as a jerk and brush aside the comments. If you do this, you may miss an opportunity to learn from the feedback.

2. **Don't interrupt.** Let the critic talk. People who are being critiqued often jump in immediately to start clarifying or justifying their actions. You don't want to cut the comments short because they may contain helpful information.

3. **Ask for details.** Sometimes people provide only generalizations when giving you feedback, such as "Your presentation didn't work." Yet to be able to learn from someone's comments, you need the person to be specific. If you are comfortable doing so, ask for more information. Questions like, "What exactly do you

mean by 'didn't work'?" or "What should I add to the presentation to improve it?" may give you clear examples of areas where you need to improve. Make sure there is no snarky tone in your voice.

4. **Paraphrase.** As mentioned elsewhere in this book, you need to check in to make sure you heard the person correctly. Saying something like, "You are suggesting that in the future I do X instead of Y" will let the person know that you understand his or her comments.

5. **Explain what happened.** Do not make excuses. However, if there were reasons for the difficulty that truly were beyond your control, calmly give the details.

6. **If you did mess up, accept responsibility.** A simple acknowledgment, such as, "I'm glad you pointed this out. I will make sure it doesn't happen again," can help to defuse a negative situation.

7. **Ask for more.** Before the conversation is over, ask for more feedback. Saying, "Tell me more . . ." or asking, "What else?" demonstrates that doing a good job is important to you. (If you believe that the person is just dumping on you, you may want to ignore this step.)

QUESTION TO CONSIDER

Q. *How do I give my colleague some feedback? She really needs help with her dress/ presentations/writing skills, etc.*

A. Giving feedback to a colleague is risky. (If you are the boss, it's part of your job.) Sometimes the person may appreciate your comments, but other times, not so much. If you truly believe that your feedback will help the person, you may choose to speak up. The key is to get the person's permission. You can ask your colleague, "Is it okay if I give you some feedback? I have some suggestions about dressing for work and thought you might like to hear them."

PRESCRIPTION FOR SUCCESS

Receiving effective feedback can be a gift, and you need to thank the person. You can simply say, "Thank you." Or "Thanks for the feedback. I appreciate it." Or "Thank you. Your comments will be very helpful to me."

56. Offended by a Comment?
Try These Simple but Powerful Responses

A woman stopped going to happy hour with her colleague after work when she heard that her colleague was telling others about her drinking habits. She didn't say anything to the coworker, but just stopped socializing with her.

Several people in my seminars have told me similar stories about quitting a job or ending a relationship after they were offended by comments made by their bosses, coworkers, or friends. But the offended workers never said anything to the people who made the objectionable comments. Unfortunately, these responses are passive.

You can step away from being passive and learn to be assertive by responding to an offensive comment without attacking the person making that comment.

Try using one of the following "polite and powerful" statements when someone makes a distasteful remark. You may be surprised at the response.

The first three ask the person to clarify his or her comments:

1. "Why are you saying that?"

2. "Help me to understand what you mean by . . ." (insert disparaging word that was used).

3. "Did you mean that as harshly as it sounded?"

The fourth statement assertively expresses your concern about the comment:

4. "I'm offended by your comment."

It is possible that the person will feel some remorse when you use any of these statements. For example, I once asked a colleague, "Why are you saying that?" after he made a negative comment about another colleague. He thought for a second and then responded, "I guess I'm just being a jerk." And that was the end of that.

If you confront someone directly, that person may stop making negative comments, or may regard you differently. Your relationship with the person may improve. (See the next chapter for more on successful confrontation.)

Of course, there is the chance that nothing you say will make a difference. But what do you have to lose by trying? Unfortunately, many people will never know. They quit their jobs or end relationships before they find out what might have happened.

PRESCRIPTION FOR SUCCESS

Sometimes you may want to acknowledge that you heard someone's comment without necessarily agreeing with or disputing the point. You can use neutral statements, such as: "That's interesting" or "That's an interesting point."

57. Stop Complaining:
Learn to Confront Others Politely

I'm getting annoyed with my coworker. She calls me "honey" all the time, and it just doesn't sit well with me. Sometimes I think that she may want more from me than just friendship. I'm not interested in a romantic relationship. I need to say something, but I don't want to offend her, so I have been avoiding her.

My husband told me, "I find it annoying that you never stand up for yourself, and then come crying to me about it." So I said, "Why haven't you told me this before?" He said he thought it would only get me more upset.

Do you speak up about the bothersome, upsetting, frustrating, or troublesome situations you encounter?

Many people don't, including the participants in my classes who are quoted above. It's not unusual. Very few people know what to say or do assertively when bothered by the behavior of others. Instead, they complain to friends or coworkers and avoid the people who bother them. Sometimes, they explode or they rant on social media. But none of these responses is likely to improve a difficult situation or help people feel good about themselves.

Fortunately, positive confrontation provides an alternative—a way for you to confront others in the "polite and powerful" manner that we have discussed. You can express what's bothering you without attacking the other person. And when you use this approach, you have the best chance of getting the result you want, and also continuing to maintain a relationship with the person.

Below are seven steps to positive confrontation. Use them as a guide to handle your own confrontations:

1. **Pick your conflict.** Some people say "pick your battles," but that's negative. Conflict is inevitable in life. You could be confronting people nonstop throughout your day, but why would you? Pick the situations that matter to you, or those that have an effect on your work. You'll be less stressed if you let the little ones go.

2. **Don't assume the person is a jerk.** We are very quick to make negative assumptions about others. If you approach someone when you are already convinced that the person is a jerk, it is very easy to explode because "the jerk had it coming!" Yet we often have no idea what is driving the other person's behavior. If you consider that the person may have a reason for acting the way he or she has, you are less likely to explode.

3. **Pick the right time and place.** You need to set the stage for a discussion. Make sure the confrontation occurs in private. It's embarrassing for other people to witness such a confrontation, and even more embarrassing for the person to whom you are speaking. You also want to confront others when you are calm. If you aren't, it is easy to say things that you will regret. Pick a time that's good for the other person. If the person is walking out the door for a meeting, it's not the time to confront him or her.

4. **Confront one issue at a time.** When you bring up a variety of issues, you can get sidetracked by the less-important ones. Plus, a person may feel that you are dumping on him or her if you bring up more than one concern at one time.

5. **Use the Don't Attack'em, WAC'em™ technique.** You should prepare what you plan to say to the other person. If you have something specific to say, you are less likely to be aggressive—or to avoid the discussion altogether.

    The key is not to attack people, but to WAC'em with your words.

    WAC is an acronym, and each letter stands for something that will help you create wording that is specific, direct, polite, and nonaccusatory. Writing your script will help you clarify your thoughts and eliminate any negative, harsh expressions.

The W stands for *What.* What is really bothering you? Define the problem. (What exactly is the person doing that annoys you?)

The A stands for *Ask.* What do you want to ask the other person to do or change? What will solve the problem? (Knowing your *A* is a very empowering step, since it means you know what you want.)

The C stands for *Check-in.* You need to check in with the other person and get his or her reaction.

For example, suppose a coworker has been posting photographs of you on Facebook without asking your permission. Here's an example of a WAC for this type of situation:

W = "I know you may not see this as a big deal, but I am not comfortable with pictures of me being posted on Facebook without my permission."

A = "Please take them down by the end of the day."

C = "Okay?"

6. **Practice.** Once you have created your wording, practice your delivery. If your words sound harsh to you, they will sound harsh to the other person. Rework your wording until you eliminate the harshness. Add polite language. You do *not* want to read your script to the other person. After practicing, you will be familiar with what you want to say, and so you'll be more likely to express yourself calmly and conversationally. And make sure your voice and body language are assertive.

7. **Be prepared for the response that follows.** When people are WACed, they may agree to what you asked of them—especially if it's reasonable. But not always. Sometimes you can get into a discussion with the person. At other times people may get defensive, or even say no. If you think ahead of time about how the person may respond, you won't be caught off guard.

PRESCRIPTION FOR SUCCESS

Don't decide to try out a WAC'em approach with short notice on a major problem. Learning new skills takes time. Start slowly. Pick simple situations to address initially, and build your confidence. Over time, you can master positive confrontation.

58. Someone Else's Bad Behavior Is No Excuse for Your Own!

A customer started to yell at the salesperson (my friend), claiming the problem they discussed earlier had not been fixed. Instead of dealing with this angry customer professionally, my friend started to yell back at him in front of other customers. Since she didn't respond calmly, my friend ended up being fired.

You have no control over how other people behave, but you *do* have control over your response to them.

A mentor told me years ago, "Someone else's bad behavior is no excuse for your own." I know that this concept can be hard to accept. Yet this viewpoint is fundamental to minimizing bad behavior in the workplace and elsewhere.

If you scream or yell back when someone is yelling at you, you are meeting that person's aggressive behavior with your own bad behavior. And meeting aggression with aggression usually makes a bad situation worse. It is rare that such behavior leads to a positive resolution—as illustrated by the negative consequence experienced by the saleswoman above who lost her job.

Also, this kind of reaction gives the other person power over you— the power to get you to lose control and become hostile, distressed, or upset. You don't want to do that!

So what do you do?

First, it is important to remember that sometimes people may be having a bad day. Any one of us can lose it, at any given time. This behavior may be an isolated incident. And you can choose to let this one go.

Second, you can respond in a polite and powerful manner. There have been many examples of assertive language in this section that may be appropriate for your situation, including saying, "I want to help, but screaming at me won't help me to help you. It will just make us both unproductive." Or asking people to clarify their comments, such as, "Did you really mean to say that so harshly?" Or using the Don't Attack'em, WAC'em technique described in the previous chapter. There are also specific tips for dealing with a bully in the next chapter.

And last but not least, you can appeal to the next level. This is not running to HR or your boss every time you don't like what someone says. But there may be situations where you need help, or you need to rely on company policy to resolve a situation. If the salesperson cited above had gone to her boss for help, she most likely would still have her job. (However, if there's ever a situation that develops where you are concerned for your safety, contact your security department promptly.)

PRESCRIPTION FOR SUCCESS

Before you react to a difficult situation, consider your own behavior. Have you done anything to contribute to the situation? Think about what you said or did. Were you rude, sarcastic, or mean-spirited? We can be very quick to blame others, and yet many times we initiate the aggression. And as mentioned above, it is then easy for the other person to respond aggressively.

59. Work with a Bully?
Tips for Asserting Yourself

A coworker asked how I spoke up after my boss made me feel foolish. I told her that "no one can make you feel inferior without your consent" [Eleanor Roosevelt's quote], and I wasn't giving the boss my consent!

This time he didn't anger me as much because I knew he was going to be a jerk, and so I prepared myself for it ahead of time.

Do you work with any bullies? These are colleagues, bosses, or employees who have strong opinions and express them aggressively without caring how their behavior affects others. They may belittle your comments, find fault with your work, put you down, yell at you, steal credit for your work, intentionally ignore you, or physically intimidate you.

Working with or for this type of person can be very unpleasant, to say the least.

You don't want to become a bully when you are interacting with one, but you do want to make sure your opinions and your work are given their due. The comments above, from participants in my seminars, illustrate how some have responded to bullies. Consider these suggestions to help disarm the bully:

Be Ready

If you know you are going to be meeting with the bully, prepare for the conversation. Review your past experiences with this person and do your homework. When you can, know what topics will be discussed. You will be less likely to be caught off guard if you have some idea what to expect. Support your opinions with facts and figures.

It is harder for others to ignore your positions if they are backed by research—though unfortunately some bullies will still try to do so.

Pay Attention to the Details

When you are cognizant of the bully's body language, his or her aggressive gestures (such as pointing or pounding) can be less intimidating. Make sure that both of you are sitting or standing. You don't want the other person towering over you. Many people look away when they get nervous. Look the person in the eye. By doing so, you are telling the other person you aren't intimidated. And raise your volume . . . a little. You don't want to yell, but you may need to speak a bit louder in order to be heard.

Don't Ask Permission to Speak

Avoid asking, "Is it okay if I give my thoughts?" The other person is not in charge of the flow of conversation. Discussions should go two ways.

Give Your Opinion as a Statement, Not a Question

You are letting the other person make the decision if you say, "Wouldn't using Vendor X be a conflict of interest for us?" Instead, use a direct, assertive statement: "Using Vendor X would be a conflict of interest."

Keep Accurate Records

Document your experiences with the bully. Write what happened. Were there any witnesses? Save any emails, texts, or notes. If you need to escalate your case to human resources, doing this will provide you with the documentation you need to support your claims.

Ask Yourself: Why Am I Staying?

By trying the above suggestions, you can feel good that you have expressed yourself and didn't back down. But at some point, if your work environment is still intolerable, you have to answer the question: Why are you staying in a place where you're working with a bully or bullies? It may be time to leave the company, or to transfer to a different department. You spend too much of your life at work to be anxious or miserable when you're there.

PRESCRIPTION FOR SUCCESS

If a situation seems in any way threatening, trust your gut. If you get a feeling that something or someone is not quite right, seek help. Talk to your boss, HR, or your security department. Better safe than sorry. The issue of safety has been raised in previous chapters, but it bears repeating: Regrettably, there are instances of workplace violence, and it's important to take care of yourself.

60. Drama Screens:
Handling Conflict Online

People will comment on a YouTube video about how good it is, and someone else will leave a comment stating how the video is stupid. The other person then gets defensive. Soon, others join in and take sides, which just stirs the proverbial pot. Then the comments turn into personal insults. Why do people act like that? It's just a YouTube video. It's like road rage, except it's online.

This comment, by one of my students, applies not just to YouTube, but to all social media. People have all sorts of fights on social media sites like Facebook, Instagram, and Twitter. People feel entitled to give their opinions, and can end up fighting with others they don't even know.

So how does this apply to the workplace?

When you post, tweet, or message someone, your comments can be seen by people you work with, or want to work with. As a result, your comments become part of your professional image.

You may have thought your colleague, whom you friended on Facebook, was a nice, pleasant person—until you saw his nasty posts on Facebook. You now believe that he is not a nice person, and this perception can affect your working relationship.

Any prospective employer most likely will check your social media sites, and if your posts indicate that you're a hothead, that you publicly put down people or your company, or that you anger others with offensive comments, why would that person want to hire you?

And your online footprint doesn't go away. What you post online may come back to haunt you, as one woman experienced when she was fired in 2013 because of a tweet. As this woman was boarding a plane to fly to South Africa, she tweeted what she thought was a joke, but others interpreted it as a racist comment. By the time her plane landed, the tweet had gone viral. Over a year later, an article in the *New York Times* magazine discussed that tweet and the consequences she and others have experienced because of their comments on social media.

Suggestions on how to avoid being confrontational online may be obvious, but they bear repeating: Think before you post—if you have any doubt about whether your comments could be offensive, don't post them. Posting negative comments about your company can be a career-limiting move. Why bite the hand that feeds you? Avoid labeling people, or their comments, as "dumb," "stupid," "idiotic," or other derogatory words. Don't get involved in other people's fights. Remember that there are usually two sides to a story (at least). And the fact that something is posted on Facebook certainly doesn't mean it's true. You can disagree with someone's comments without being nasty yourself. Finally, shut down heated exchanges by disengaging from the conversation. If someone is consistently a problem because of contentious or inappropriate posts, you can block, hide, or unfollow that person.

PRESCRIPTION FOR SUCCESS

Take the conversation offline. Social media is not the place to work out a disagreement with someone you know well. Sometimes calling the person, or meeting face-to-face with the person in a public, safe, and neutral place, can help both parties resolve their differences. (For your own safety, however, do not meet one-on-one with people you know only online.)

61. Staying Festive: Ways to Avoid Conflict at the Holidays

One young man drank too much at his company's holiday party, cursed out his boss, and was fired on the spot.

A woman did not respond to an invitation to a colleague's holiday dinner party. She showed up at the party, but it was awkward for the host, who had to quickly set up another place setting.

The holiday season can bring lots of opportunities for gift-giving, party-going, and joyful celebrating. But as the above comments from some of my seminar participants illustrate, there are also lots of opportunities for embarrassing situations and conflict.

In my assertiveness seminars, I ask people to discuss their conflicts. Many involve the holidays, and these conflicts drive people crazy because it is already a stressful time of year. Review this list and make sure you are aware of these "polite and powerful" ways to reduce the likelihood of holiday conflict:

1. **Don't become a holiday slacker.** Coworkers who take three-hour lunches to finish holiday shopping, or who call in sick to avoid working the holiday, make the holidays more stressful for their coworkers. This kind of behavior can really annoy people. The old Golden Rule still applies during this time of the year—treat others as you would want to be treated.

2. **Participate.** Don't be the person who refuses to celebrate or get into the holiday spirit. People who constantly complain about the holidays cause stress for everyone around them. You don't want to be labeled as a Scrooge. Attend the party hosted by your

department or your company. Participate in group gifts, when possible. Wish people "Happy Holidays."

3. **Stay sober.** A lot of liquor can be served at celebrations during the holidays, and sometimes people drink too much. When this happens, they are more likely to say and do things that cause problems for themselves and others—as the young man mentioned above experienced. Limit your alcohol intake, and your holiday celebrating is less likely to become a problem.

4. **Respond to RSVPs.** Failing to respond to an invitation that requests a reply and then showing up at the event, or saying that you will attend and then *not* showing up, is inconsiderate. Both behaviors are likely to cause problems for the host. Always reply to an invitation, whether it is to accept or to decline. If you accept, but an unavoidable conflict develops, preventing you from attending, call (do not text) the host and explain. (Note that a more desirable invitation does not qualify as "unavoidable conflict." The invitation you accepted first takes precedence.)

5. **Don't post inappropriate photos on social media.** When people are celebrating, some of them may get carried away and post photos from parties or other events that are not public. Often, the people being tagged in those photos would prefer that the images remain private. To avoid online conflict, err on the side of caution. Ask the people in your photos if it's okay to post them. When in doubt, don't put the photos out there.

6. **Avoid gift-giving gaffes.** Gifts are supposed to make people feel good, but unfortunately gift-giving can cause a lot of problems. People who give inappropriate gifts to others—such as items that are too personal for coworkers—may cause conflict at work. Know what is appropriate for your workplace. Plus, make sure you show appreciation for any gift you receive, even if you don't like it. Say thank you, and also write thank you notes.

7. **Remember the true meaning of the holidays.** With Black Friday, Small Business Saturday, and Cyber Monday, it's easy to think

that the holidays are all about material things. Those who focus on giving to others, being with family and friends, and doing nice things for other people are most likely to enjoy the holidays with the least amount of conflict.

PRESCRIPTION FOR SUCCESS

Your colleagues will often celebrate different holidays. Wishing people "Happy Holidays" will apply to everyone, regardless of their religious or cultural affiliations. If you know for sure that a person celebrates a certain holiday, you can reference that specific one, such as "Merry Christmas" or "Happy Hanukkah."

PART IV

IT'S YOUR RESPONSIBILITY: CAREER ADVANCEMENT AND JOB SEARCH

Your actions—good and bad—will have an impact on your career. Sometimes the impact may be subtle, but at other times it will be quite clear where you made a good move or had a misstep.

Consider these two scenarios and their outcomes:

- A boss emailed an employee that he would have to move his desk as a result of office restructuring. The employee, reluctant to move, fired back this response: "Hell, no. I'm not doing that!" The man was demoted.

- One woman took all the right steps to land her dream job:

    This job started with an introduction by a mutual acquaintance, followed by a phone interview with the person I met, then lunch at a local restaurant, then two in-person interviews, and then the interview with the CEO. Fairly lengthy process, but it paid off. I got the job.

How your career progresses is largely up to you, so resolve now to take responsibility for it and make it the best you can.

This section contains information on how to build your career in a professional manner, from the time you start looking for work. Putting these suggestions into practice will have a positive impact on your daily behavior, your attitude about your career, and your long-term plans for your profession.

62. Your Career Is What You Make It— So Make It Something!

I never really thought that I had to plan my career. I took the first job I was offered and just thought things would materialize. They didn't.

Successful careers don't happen overnight. Well, there is always the exception, such as the understudy who fills in for the Broadway star on opening night . . . and you know the rest of the story. But most of us, as the above quote illustrates, need to take deliberate steps to develop our careers.

The following career-development suggestions are helpful for those just starting in the workplace, but many of the tips also apply to more-seasoned professionals.

1. **Take responsibility for your career.** Just because you have a job, it doesn't mean that you can stop thinking about your future. You are likely to be working for quite a few years, so you want to think strategically about the long term. As author Lewis Carroll said, "If you don't know where you are going, any road will get you there." You want to be aware of your career possibilities and put yourself on the road toward your goal.

2. **Develop an area of expertise within your profession.** Start building your reputation. In what category do you want to become known as an expert? You don't have to make a decision right away, but be open to finding areas that you might enjoy, and where you are likely to grow and excel.

3. **Evaluate whether you will need additional schooling.** Do you need any certifications to advance in your field? Will an additional degree be beneficial? Can you take advantage of any company college reimbursement programs? If your company will pay for part or

all of a bachelor's or master's degree, why not take advantage of this opportunity? One woman I coached had gotten both degrees with reimbursement help from her employer, and was now leading a large division of her company. Know what you need, and what's available to you.

4. **Build your network.** A network of supportive professionals is a valuable resource. Your network shouldn't be made up exclusively of people in your field. They may be a substantial part of your network, but people from other professions and walks of life should be included. Additional information on building a network can be found in Chapter 67.

5. **Find a mentor.** It's important to have people you can count on and learn from as you advance in your career. A mentor is someone you know personally, and he or she will take an active role in your development. Some companies have formal mentoring programs—sign up for such a program if you can. If not, develop a relationship with a more experienced individual informally over time.

6. **Remember that sometimes a bad job can provide great experience.** Think about what you are gaining from the position. You may not like your daily activities, but you could be gaining the skills you need to move up within your company, or qualifications that equip you to apply for a better position elsewhere.

7. **Follow your "bliss."** People may find that what they studied in school, or the field in which they are working, no longer interests them. Sometimes people discover their real career passion only after working for a few years. Carefully consider your possibilities, and be open to making a change. Actor Hugh Jackman mentions following his "bliss" when he took what became his award-winning role in the Broadway show *The Boy from Oz*. He said in an interview in *Southwest* magazine: "It wasn't what anyone considered a good career move, but I just knew it was the right thing to do."

QUESTION TO CONSIDER

Q. *My boss keeps giving me more assignments. He isn't paying me enough to do all this stuff. What do I do?*

A. Change your mindset. You can view the assignments as a way of getting more experience. You can talk to your boss about your job responsibilities and how you spend your time. You can ask for a raise, since your responsibilities have increased. Or you can get your résumé together and look for another position. Don't make yourself a victim — you most likely have options.

PRESCRIPTION FOR SUCCESS

As you plan your career, it's also important not to overlook your retirement. Start building your financial future as early as you can. Take advantage of any retirement plans your company offers. Saving even a little amount from each paycheck now will make a significant difference to you when you retire, because those small amounts will grow over time.

63. Build Your Career,
One Day at a Time

I never knew there was so much to do!

A young graduate said this to me during our coaching session. He had never really thought much about how to develop his career.

Career development is an ongoing process. You always want to create and take advantage of opportunities, get noticed, develop your skills, and establish relationships. The previous chapter spoke about the broader picture of building a career. The following suggestions have a different focus, as they relate directly to your day-to-day performance.

1. **Have "fire in your belly."** This means that you have a powerful sense of determination—of working hard to succeed. Some people seem to be born with this attribute; others have to create it. To ignite that blaze, go above and beyond. Do more than what is expected of you. Show initiative. If you say you are going to do something, do it. Meet or beat your deadlines. When you can, solve problems. Convey enthusiasm for your work. Get to work early, and don't rush out the door at the end of the day. Wouldn't you want to hire or promote someone who has this work ethic? I would.

2. **Do good work.** Sloppy or inferior work is not acceptable. Quality counts. Pay attention to details. Stay abreast of any new trends in your field. And apply everything you have learned so far—communicate competently with colleagues, bosses, and customers; send emails without mistakes; and make presentations skillfully.

3. **Get to know your coworkers.** You don't need to know their life stories, but knowing a little about their lives will help you connect with them. Let them know a little about you, too. People want to work with others that they like and trust.

4. **Wear appropriate attire.** What you wear can either enhance people's opinions of your professionalism or detract from it. If you want people to see you as a professional, dress like one.

5. **Don't burn your bridges.** If you are nasty to people or unprofessional in your work, your reputation will suffer. Many professions are "small worlds," and you can be sure that people you work with know people in your field. When you apply for a new position, your reputation will follow you—or precede you. One manager said that his employee, when leaving the company, was so inconsiderate of his coworkers that he would never give that employee a reference.

PRESCRIPTION FOR SUCCESS

Do not sneak out when leaving work. Say goodbye to your colleagues and add an exit line, such as, "Have a good night," or "See you tomorrow," or "Have a safe trip home." And if appropriate for your situation, you might say to the boss, "I'm getting ready to go. Do you need me to do anything before I close up shop / shut things down / leave for the night?"

64. Seven Tips for Young Women Just Starting Their Careers

A newly appointed vice president said that she had never thought about becoming a CEO until her mentor told her, "You could be running this place in a few years."

A college student decided to abandon her dream job of becoming a physician because she wanted to "have a life." She hoped to marry and have children, and thought that she couldn't have a successful family life as well as a career as a doctor.

A young woman became all-but-invisible in her office because she rarely voiced her opinion. On the rare occasion that she did say something, she spoke so softly that no one heard her.

The (formerly) successful businesswoman said, "My husband does very well. I don't have to work." Yet she was bored at home and missed the challenges she had encountered at work.

Though the examples above touch on very different scenarios, they highlight how women can hobble themselves—often unintentionally—and restrict their careers through their own actions.

There has been a lot of interest in recent years centered on helping women to succeed in the workplace. Among the more high-profile endeavors were MSNBC's Mika Brzezinski's efforts to empower women via her Know Your Value national tour, based on her book of the same name. Through her book, *Lean In*, a related website, and ongoing updates in the media, Facebook chief operating officer Sheryl Sandberg encourages young girls and women to "lean in" to their ambitions and to speak up so their voices are heard.

I applaud these efforts and others like them, as many of the career-limiting factors that I began speaking about more than 20 years ago are still evident today and affecting a new generation of young women. Although women have to overcome many obstacles in the workplace, unnecessary hurdles are often erected by women themselves. Before women can take control of their lives and their careers, they have to recognize what they are doing to handicap themselves.

Here are some suggestions for overcoming career barriers:

1. **Don't limit yourself.** Be open to opportunities. Aim high. More and more women are advancing in the workplace, and you can be one of them. The vice president mentioned earlier in the chapter explained that once her mentor expressed the possibility of her advancement, she began thinking that she could become the CEO of her company.

2. **Don't limit your options based on an unknown future.** Why put restrictions on your career choices when no one knows what the future will hold? You don't know what your life will be like in five or ten years. I know a number of career women, including physicians, who successfully balance having children and a career. If you are smart enough to advance, you will be smart enough to find solutions to your concerns.

3. **Overcome roadblocks.** Many times people will tell you that you can't do something or that things can't be done a certain way. Sometimes that may be true, but not always! Often, roadblocks turn out to be mere stumbling blocks that you can overcome. When I decided to go to graduate school, several friends told me it was too late to apply. Despite what they thought, I carried my papers from department to department, explained my case, and started my master's program on time.

4. **Appreciate history.** Learn about the struggles of women in the past. Had it not been for the efforts of women before you, many of the opportunities that you have today wouldn't exist. Don't take these new possibilities for granted. Oprah Winfrey said, "I have crossed over on the backs of Sojourner Truth and Harriet

Tubman and Fannie Lou Hamer and Madam C.J. Walker. Because of them I can now live the dream. I am the seed of the free, and I know it. I intend to bear great fruit."

5. **Learn from others.** How have other successful women overcome their challenges, and how can you incorporate their solutions into your career and life? A woman in one of my seminars had four young sons, worked full time, and still found the time to earn her MBA. To help manage family and career, she had a to-do list that included weekly family meetings to discuss the upcoming week's activities. Her idea has helped many others. Remember there is no one perfect career path that fits everyone. Do your research and find what works for you.

6. **Support and encourage your friends and colleagues.** Madeleine Albright, the first female U.S. Secretary of State, said, "There is a special place in hell for women who don't help other women." Sometimes, telling a colleague, "You can do it!" will encourage her to go back to school. Helping a friend out when she needs an emergency babysitter may allow her to attend her night class. Remember, there's truth to the saying, "What goes around, comes around."

7. **Embrace your strengths.** Identify what you excel at or enjoy doing. Work on developing those areas. You are more likely to succeed if you enjoy your work. If you aren't sure of your strengths, consult with a trusted colleague or your network, or review your performance appraisals.

PRESCRIPTION FOR SUCCESS

Pick the father of your children wisely. Once you have children, life gets more complicated. You will want someone who is a partner in every sense, someone who supports you and your career. Sometimes people say the right things; make sure your partner truly believes them.

65. Many People Are Giving Me Career Suggestions. What Do I Do?

A young woman was told by a supervisor that her giggle during her presentation was cute, and fit her personality.

A woman asked her husband if her skirt was too short for an important business meeting, and he responded "No, your legs look great. Keep it short!"

A young man was told by a colleague to chew gum to help him overcome his nervousness when speaking in public.

As you advance in your career, people are likely to offer suggestions to try to help you. Sometimes, you may be asking for the person's help. Other times, the comments may be unsolicited. Either way, it is important to evaluate the suggestions.

Consider the three individuals above and the advice they received. Do you believe the comments were helpful to my seminar participants? I believe these business professionals all received feedback that was flawed.

To decide which suggestions might help you to grow as a professional and which ones to ignore, ask yourself these questions:

1. **Who is giving the feedback?** Is the person an expert? If so, I would seriously consider following the person's suggestions. If the person is not an expert, I would put the comments on the back burner. But remember, when customers make suggestions, it is a good idea to implement them when and where appropriate.

2. **Do you notice a pattern?** One person's opinion may not carry much weight, but a series of similar comments from a variety of people likely signals valid criticism—positive or negative. In that case, think seriously about what you were told. Oliver Burkeman,

writing in *The Guardian* newspaper about Heidi Grant Halvor-son's book *No One Understands You and What to Do About It*, clearly explained the importance of patterns:

> *When it comes to judging how people see you, trust the numbers. Our individual encounters with each other may be distorted by bias and egocentrism, but in aggregate, patterns emerge. . . . It may be true that nobody understands you, but when they all don't understand you in exactly the same way, there's probably a lesson lurking there.*

3. **Do you understand the comments?** Make sure you grasp what the person is actually saying. The young woman who was told it was okay to giggle could have asked, "Are you saying that it will be professional for me to giggle in the business world?" (The answer is no!) Perhaps the supervisor didn't know how to give critical feedback.

4. **Do the comments emphasize your sexuality?** Workplace feedback should address your competency, not your sexuality. The woman's husband in my example was flattering his wife, but not taking into consideration her corporate environment. He didn't understand that "sexy is not a corporate look." He's not alone. Considering the attire of some newscasters, or the actors portraying professionals on television shows, it's not surprising that many people come to believe that it is okay to dress provocatively in business situations. Occasionally, even some people writing about dress guidelines on the web fall into this trap. One blog post I read suggested that showing cleavage is the new "power tie" for women. It isn't!

PRESCRIPTION FOR SUCCESS

If you have any doubts about suggestions you receive, check with other seasoned and successful professionals. The young man who was told to chew gum checked with another professional who pointed out that the gum chewing would distract his audience. She then gave him other suggestions to overcome his nervousness, such as practicing out loud and telling himself positive things.

66. Don't Put Yourself Down—
Speak Well of Yourself Instead

Nell, a fictional intelligence analyst on the TV show NCIS: Los
Angeles, *said to her assistant director: "Thank you for letting me tag along today. I just hope I didn't get in the way or
anything, sir."*

The assistant director responded: "Don't do that."

Nell: "Excuse me?"

*Assistant director: "I didn't let you tag along today. I brought
you with me because I needed backup and you have field experience. Never belittle yourself or your accomplishments. You
deserve the respect you got. You earned it."*

When you put yourself down, you make it easy for others not to take
you or your work seriously. Learning to speak well of yourself is an
important aspect of building your career and your reputation.

Some people may put themselves down because they are unsure of
themselves and want reassurance. This rationale may have prompted
Nell's comments. Instead of discounting herself, however, she could have
said, "I'm still new to being out in the field. Any suggestions for me?"

Others don't speak well of themselves because they believe it will
be viewed as bragging, which is flaunting one's accomplishments so
much that it comes across as obnoxious boasting. While bragging is
not the way to impress colleagues or bosses, speaking well of yourself
is important to do.

Learn to stop belittling yourself and highlight your accomplishments, without being off-putting, by applying these suggestions:

Monitor Your Comments

Review what you say about yourself in your conversations with others. If you put yourself down, think about what you could have said instead. Analyze people's responses to your comments. Are they similar to what Nell's assistant director said to her? You can't change your behavior until you become aware that you are doing something that needs changing.

Don't Advertise Your Inexperience

When people start a new job, they frequently say, "I've never done this before" or "Um, this is all new for me." When you are just learning a new job, you can't know everything all at once, and your new colleagues usually realize that. Yet you want people to view you as a capable, competent person. Reminding them of your inexperience creates a different image.

Be Prepared

Know ahead of time how you will introduce yourself to others. This can occur when you go to a networking event, are a new member of a group, or are in a meeting when everyone in the room introduces him- or herself. Keep your comments simple and positive, such as: "I'm Tom Smith, the new manager in sales. Jake Jones brought me in to start the new quality project. I'm very excited about this opportunity and look forward to working with you all."

When Asked, Do Tell

Have you ever asked someone, "How's work?" And the person responds, "Oh, everything's fine." But later you find out that this coworker had just been accepted into a prestigious management training program. You have to wonder, "Why didn't he tell me!" When someone asks, it is usually a good time to tell that person of your new accomplishments.

Have Your Awards Speak for You

Winning professional or community awards builds your credibility and can be an important way to promote yourself. To be eligible for many awards, other people have to recommend you; for some, however, you can nominate yourself. This is not an obnoxious thing to do. You still have to earn the award.

Speak Well of Yourself on Your Social Media Sites

Occasionally, posting your accomplishments is a quick and easy way to let people know about your successes. Most of your online friends would be interested if you won an award, received a promotion, or got accepted into graduate school. Recruiters or potential employers also may see these accomplishments. Just don't overdo these postings.

PRESCRIPTION FOR SUCCESS

Avoid the technique known as "humblebrag" — its practitioners still brag, but try to disguise it as being humble or mildly self-deprecating. This is usually achieved by admitting to a minor flaw while really drawing attention to the big-brag item. My favorite example of this is, "I am such a klutz. I just spilled wine on my new book contract." Avoid this clearly phony approach in conversation as well as in social media postings. If you've achieved something you feel is really praiseworthy, own it honestly.

67. Build Your Network
Both Online and Off

I needed help in deciding whether to accept a job offer. I asked people in my network who were familiar with the company. One of them had worked for my potential new boss and provided great insight. I took the job.

Having a network is not optional. It is essential for a successful career, because members of your network may assist you when it comes to switching jobs, give you help and advice, help you to build your reputation, keep you abreast of professional trends, and even enable you to sell more of your services or products.

But networking is not a one-way street. People will help you, and you need to help them too. Become a resource for people. If you can, help them find solutions to their problems. The most effective networks consist of individuals who are genuinely interested in one another as colleagues and human beings.

So how do you meet people to include in your network?

The answer is relatively simple: Keep an open mind. You are most likely interacting with people every day who could be part of your network. You just need to be willing to put yourself out there and get involved—both online and off.

Online networks can be very effective when researching new contacts, for giving others an overview of your strengths, and for maintaining contact with people. But online activities do not replace face-to-face interactions. You still need to meet with people to develop relationships fully. Make sure you do the following:

1. **Get out of your office.** Join colleagues for lunch. Get to know them and let them know you. Many people work from home or do all their work online and don't see colleagues daily. You need to make

an effort to meet with people to get a more complete picture of who they are. Attend business and social functions—this means holiday, retirement, and birthday parties, and other company celebrations. You don't need to go to every event, but you do need to attend when you can.

2. **Join professional associations.** Get involved. Go to meetings. Attend annual conferences if possible. Become a member of a committee. Run for office. Doing these things will allow you to learn about your profession and meet people who share your interest in your field. Associations can be extremely important building blocks for your career.

3. **Get involved in activities at your organization.** Join company teams. You don't have to be a great athlete. Just get out there and have fun. Some companies also have on-site clubs where you can learn or improve your skills. Many companies sponsor charitable activities. If yours does, sign up. Not only will you be helping a good cause; you will be meeting new people.

4. **Be up-to-date with your network on social media.** Congratulate your contacts on their achievements and send them birthday greetings. Comment on their posts and retweet their tweets, if appropriate. Join groups and build your network on LinkedIn. Just remember, everything you post, including photographs and comments, should be suitable for the business world.

5. **Get involved in your alumni network.** Many such groups offer mixers, seminars, and career services. Becoming part of these groups can help you reconnect with old friends and meet new ones.

6. **Join community clubs, participate in sports leagues, and volunteer at charitable organizations.** Many cities have numerous cultural and sporting activities. Find some that interest you and get involved. A colleague of mine moved to a new city and met many people for his network by joining a community volleyball league.

7. **Make connections for others.** People in your network may be able to help each other. You can start that process by making an intro-

duction when there is a possible benefit to both individuals. An introduction can be done in person, via email, or through LinkedIn.

8. **Send notes to express appreciation, sympathy, or concern for someone.** Email is the quick and easy way to do this. If you are connected with the person on social media, sending a message on Facebook or a direct message on Twitter can also work. Handwritten notes stand out. You don't have to write a lot, but a few sentences wishing a colleague a speedy recovery after a serious illness can be a memorable kindness.

QUESTION TO CONSIDER

Q. *Someone in my network was laid off. What should I do?*

A. Contact the person and offer to help, if you can. Meet with him or her if possible. Let the person know of any openings you are aware of, and offer to make introductions to people who could be helpful. You can write a personal note in a card, or send a message via email or LinkedIn.

PRESCRIPTION FOR SUCCESS

Learn to mingle. Many people become uncomfortable when socializing and will not attend networking events as a result. Socializing doesn't come naturally to everyone, but the skills can be mastered by anyone—even the very shy. Here are some key suggestions to get you started: Walk into a room like you belong there. Have good posture and dress appropriately. Show interest through your body language, by looking pleasant and not crossing your arms. Don't stand by yourself or text others. Introduce yourself to someone who is by him- or herself. Shake hands correctly. Ask the person a question to get a conversation started. The more you attend events and practice mingling, the more comfortable you will become.

68. Are You Letting Networking Opportunities Pass You By?

*I introduced myself to the person sitting next to me at my asso-
ciation meeting. She started talking to me and asked, "What
do you do?" I replied, "I'm new to the area and looking for
work." Long story short, it turned out her company had an
opening—and I got the job.*

Are you taking advantage of all the interactions that occur between
people every day that can be networking opportunities?

The woman in that introductory anecdote was me, and I strongly
believe that by introducing myself to the woman sitting next to me,
I found a job.

The last chapter talked about the overall picture of networking.
Take the following self-assessment to find out if you are paying attention to the daily exchanges that can occur between people. Of course,
all these activities won't lead to job offers, but many of them may add
interesting, helpful people to your network.

	Yes	No
1. Do you introduce yourself to the people on either side of you when you take your seat at a meeting?	❏	❏
2. Did you approach a "stranger" at your organization's last social event?	❏	❏
3. Do you say hello to people you don't know when you're waiting in line?	❏	❏
4. When eating lunch in the cafeteria, have you joined people you didn't know?	❏	❏
5. If someone asks for your business card, are you always prepared?	❏	❏

	Yes	No
6. Do you ask questions to encourage people to talk?	❑	❑
7. Do you mingle with people other than those you know when attending a networking event?	❑	❑
8. Are you allowing yourself to meet more people by attending networking events on your own?	❑	❑
9. When someone says, "Give me a call" or "Let's get together," do you follow up?	❑	❑

As you have probably guessed by now, you should have answered yes to all of these questions. If you didn't, you are probably letting some terrific opportunities slip away. Be open to networking possibilities. Make a note to pay attention to your weak areas and work on improving them.

Exercise

Prepare a daily "conversation starter"—an opening line that can be used to help start a conversation. This line is a general statement or question based on noncontroversial current events or the activity in which you are participating. You can use the same conversation starter throughout your day as you meet different people. Examples include: "Did the bad weather affect your commute?" Or "Did you watch the playoffs last night?" Or "Looks like everyone has been busy around here."

PRESCRIPTION FOR SUCCESS

If you feel nervous practicing any of the above suggestions, you can tell yourself it is your job to help others feel more comfortable. This is the role the host plays at any event. It is amazing how much more open you are to other people when you adopt this role.

69. How to "Keep in Touch" Professionally and Successfully

My vice president asked me to stay in touch. How do I do that?

A client and a reader of my blog both had higher-ups in their companies tell them to "keep in touch." Both believe these individuals were sincere in their requests, so they wanted to know the best way to maintain these important career relationships.

They were right to inquire because a delicate balance is required to "keep in touch" successfully. You do not want to be a pest, but you don't want the higher-ups to forget you, either.

The following list contains a number of suggestions for keeping connections alive. Do not, of course, do all of them at once! The general guideline would be to implement any one of these about once a quarter. Depending on your relationship with the person, or any special reason for maintaining contact, you might need to reach out more or less frequently.

1. **Email any updates** about promotions, new assignments, unusual business travel, or nonwork activities of interest. Keep the message short and upbeat. For example, a vendor sent me an email saying she had been selected to compete in an international sporting event. It was great to hear of her success.

2. **Forward articles of interest.** If you come across an unusual article on a topic of mutual interest that the person may not have seen, send it to him or her. The Internet makes this very easy to do.

3. **Use social media.** There is a lot you can do if the "keep in touch" person participates in social media, as discussed throughout this book. Be careful with Facebook. If the "keep in touch" person wants to friend you, make sure your Facebook page is business-

appropriate before responding. (But don't initiate a friend request.) If you have a professional blog, let the person know of it—it can be a great way to maintain regular contact. Some higher-ups participate on LinkedIn. If a senior person asks you to "stay in touch," you can initiate a LinkedIn connection.

4. **Ask for advice or suggestions.** Asking someone's opinion can be very flattering to the person. Make sure it's a worthy request, not something trivial. This can be done in person or by email.

5. **Informally "stop by."** Do this infrequently, and have a legitimate reason for doing so. You can say something like, "I was in the building for a meeting and thought I would stop and say hi." Judge how long you should stay by the response you receive. If the person invites you into the office, it usually means he or she has time to talk. If not, it's usually best to keep the conversation short.

6. **Invite the person to coffee or lunch.** Make sure you have a strong-enough relationship for this one. One salesperson in my seminars would invite her "keep in touch" person to lunch during her annual visit to the home office. She emailed the person ahead of time to set up the appointment.

PRESCRIPTION FOR SUCCESS

Send holiday cards. The old standard of mailing cards is still a good way to stay in touch. Include a handwritten comment, such as "Tom, thanks for all your help this year." You can also email virtual greeting cards. Make sure to include a personal note with the e-card, as well.

70. Don't Whine About Your Job. Do Something!

My coworker hates her job and she keeps complaining to me. I have tried to talk to her about what she could do, but she is not listening.

My husband keeps threatening to quit his job. He only comments negatively about his job and the people who work with him. I wish he would just do something.

My friend was having difficulty with her schedule, but she didn't go to her boss to discuss alternatives. She just quit. When I had a problem, my boss adjusted my schedule. My friend's might have been adjusted, too, if she had said something.

As these comments from participants in my seminars indicate, tackling problems that affect our work lives can be difficult.

When some people become dissatisfied with their jobs, they do nothing. Perhaps they don't know how to proceed, or maybe they don't believe there is anything they can do to improve the situation. Usually, the only action they take is to whine about their bosses, their colleagues, or the work. Unfortunately, complaining doesn't accomplish anything—except having your friends, colleagues, and others stay clear of you.

Some, on the other hand, get so frustrated that they impulsively quit their jobs without having another lined up, or without a plan for the future.

Both reactions can affect your career negatively. However, there are alternatives that can help people evaluate their work situations. Answering the following four questions encourages people to take action and decide their next steps.

1. **Ask yourself, what is the real issue?** It is easy to say, "I hate my job," but it is important to identify why. What is the real issue that is causing you to be unhappy? Be honest and be specific. Is it the type of work you do, or just one aspect of the job? Is it the commute, the money, your boss, the people you work with, or any number of other causes? One man I coached liked most facets of his job, but he wanted to quit because he had to make frequent presentations. Another realized that her new position involved using unfamiliar technology, which made her feel uncomfortable and unqualified.

2. **Can you solve the problem?** Now that you have identified the issue, is there something that can be done? Is there a realistic solution? If so, what do you have to lose by asking for it? Make the case for your suggestion, including any benefits to your department or to the company. One woman realized that she liked her job, but it was the commute that was driving her crazy. She asked her boss if she could work from home two days a week. Once she assured her boss that her productivity wouldn't be affected, she was successful in having her schedule changed. Remember that if you don't speak up, chances are nothing will change.

3. **Are there advantages to this job?** If you can't solve the problem, think about what you are gaining from the position. Don't just quickly say, "Nothing." Here are four possible things to consider:

   - Is the job a stepping-stone? Will you need the skills you gain from this position to qualify for a job on the next rung of the ladder?

   - Is there any education or training perk to which you have access? Some companies will fund part or all of your ongoing education. This can be a major benefit for many people.

   - Whom are you meeting? Does the job allow you to interact with people and build your network? If so, it is possible that by having a strong network, additional job opportunities will come your way.

- Can you learn to manage your boss? Learning to work with difficult people is an important skill that almost certainly will be beneficial to you at some point in your career.

4. **Is it time to start a job search?** Depending on how you answer the questions above, you may decide that it is time to start looking for a new position. You may even decide to change careers. Any number of alternatives may now be available to you. This doesn't mean you just quit your job. Generally, it is best to look for a new job (or career) while you are still working at the old one. (Read more about looking for work in the following chapters.)

Whether you decide to stay at your current job or to look for a new one, feel good about your choice. You are doing something. You no longer need to whine.

PRESCRIPTION FOR SUCCESS

Discover whether you are a whiner. After talking with a friend, review your conversation. Did you do most of the talking about your "lousy" job, boss, or coworkers? Or ask a trusted friend whether you complain about your job a lot in conversation. If the answer is yes, address the situation. Periodically review the questions in this chapter to make sure you aren't backsliding.

71. How Do I Conduct a Job Search? Suggestions for Success

Great article about subtle actions that ruin your job search. I display 4 items that you listed (not paying attention to details, not communicating well, not connecting well with others, and never offering any help). As a result, I am unemployed.

This comment, posted online about one of my articles, highlights the consequences of ignoring some of the numerous items that are part of a job search. There are so many items that I have sorted them into three distinct categories:

1. The Approach
2. The Groundwork
3. The Daily Activities

The Approach

These details help you to develop a job-search mindset.

1. **Spend time on your search.** You want to do an exhaustive search to ensure that you don't miss any openings. If you are unemployed, view your search as a full-time job. If you are employed, set aside time for your search.

2. **Don't throw in the towel.** You may not get job offers, or you may get offers for jobs you don't want. It can become easy to ask, "Why bother?" and give up your search, but don't do that! It may take some time, but job seekers who are persistent are more likely to succeed.

3. **Don't stop looking until your job offer is official.** When you think that you are about to get an offer, you may want to stop your

search. Avoid doing this at all costs. The offer may not happen, and you will have lost time and possibly other offers.

4. **Be a resource for others.** Let a job seeker know if you learn of a suitable opening. When you help others, they are more likely to help you.

The Groundwork

These are the details you need to pay attention to as you get ready for your search. Some may be little things, but they can have an impact. One supervisor said, "When calling candidates to set up an interview, I will not leave a message (nor call back later) if the voice mail message that I hear is unprofessional."

1. **Get organized.** Designate a private and quiet space for your search. Keeping good notes will be critical. There will be a lot to keep track of once you start your search, including names, actions you need to take, and information to remember about companies and individuals.

2. **Create or update your résumé and cover letter.** You will need both for most job openings. The next chapter contains specifics for each of them.

3. **Google yourself.** Know what people will find when they look you up. If something appears that might damage your reputation and/or your ability to get hired, consider consulting a "reputation management specialist" to help control what people see about you. Search LinkedIn or Google to find these specialists. Set up a Google alert for your name (www.google.com/alert), which will notify you when something containing your name appears online.

4. **Answer your phone professionally.** Let people know to whom they are speaking—use a greeting and state your first and last names. ("Hello, Kelly Jones speaking.") Have an appropriate voice mail message, also. ("Hello, you have reached Kelly Jones. Please leave your message.")

5. **Attend to email basics.** Make sure your name is identifiable in your email address, as you want a prospective employer to know who sent it. Include your contact information in your email signature.

6. **Have current business cards.** Always carry business cards with you. You never know when you may encounter someone to whom you want to give one. Your cards should be in good shape and readily available.

7. **Stay focused.** It is easy to put off your job search. To overcome this, set a number of activities, both online and off, to achieve each week. Work toward meeting that goal and be accountable to someone—it will make you more likely to meet your target. Check in with this person periodically. You can also hire a career coach.

8. **Take care of yourself.** A job search can be stressful. Make sure you stay fit and well rested to minimize the stress. Keep a positive attitude.

The Daily Activities

Now that we've gone over the preparation for your search, it's time to begin actively seeking and applying for jobs. Once again, there are many steps that can help you reach your desired goal. They include:

1. **Let people know you are looking.** This action is number one for a reason. More people get jobs through networking than any other way. Your friends, colleagues, acquaintances, and friends of friends can't help you unless they know you're looking. Attend networking events. Continue your involvement in your professional and community activities. (Review Chapters 67 and 68 for ways to interact with your network.)

2. **Use social media.** Many people use social media to find out what is available in their field and to apply for jobs. (However, be cautious if your bosses are among your online connections.) These sites are also invaluable for allowing prospective employers to

discover your credentials. But there is more you can do to improve your chances:

- Make sure you are constantly building your online network. You don't want to start this when you are unemployed.

- LinkedIn has a free job-search option that can be very helpful. (My son got his first full-time job this way.) It also has a paid option that provides additional resources. Make sure your profile is complete—including a professional photograph and recommendations. You can politely message people who work for companies you have an interest in. Sometimes they will provide helpful information, or even tell you of possible openings.

- Use Twitter to follow people, including recruiters and companies you would like to work for. Respond to their tweets. Many companies tweet about job openings.

- Learn about companies by following their Instagram accounts. Instagram also can let prospective employers see your creative side through your postings.

3. **Apply to postings on websites.** These include:

- Company sites that list their openings, such as wawa.com/careers.aspx. Some companies will send you job alerts.

- Online job sites, such as indeed.com, careerbuilder.com, or simplyhired.com. These sites have thousands of job listings from around the country.

- Specialized sites that concentrate on one profession, such as lawjobs.com.

- Job boards from your professional associations. You don't always have to be a member of the association to explore the postings.

- Sites your colleagues have used successfully. Ask people in your network what has been helpful for them.

4. **Take advantage of what your college has to offer.** Use its Career Center and attend Career Fairs. Don't forget the importance of getting involved in your alumni network too.

5. **Investigate recruiters.** If you can, develop a relationship with a recruiter. He or she will expose you to career opportunities that you might not know about otherwise. Though recruiters typically work on more senior, higher-paying positions, your network may help you find a suitable one. Recruiters also may find you through your LinkedIn account.

6. **Explore possibilities within your company.** Are there other positions with your current employer that interest you? Why not apply for them? Also, if you have a network within your company, you may learn about openings before they are posted.

7. **Evaluate your choices.** As we mentioned earlier, you may get an offer for a position that isn't exactly what you wanted. Taking this job may get you back into the workplace after an absence, or it may provide an opportunity to learn skills you need. One lawyer summed it up best:

> *You said that where you start is not necessarily where you wind up. You were right. After my three-year hiatus, I returned to work in a part-time capacity with a specific focus on one line of business, and now, less than a year later, I am running the entire show.*

Exercise

Read one article a day about job hunting. Keep a list of any tips you find that you may be able to use. There is an amazing amount of information on the web to help you and keep you focused on your search.

PRESCRIPTION FOR SUCCESS

Post your résumé as soon as you see an opening in which you are interested. Many postings receive lots of responses, and companies may stop reviewing résumés after a certain number have come in — even though the listing is still "open."

72. Perk Up Your Résumé and Cover Letter

While in the process of reviewing résumés, I came across one with a few typos. I do understand that people make mistakes, but as this was my first impression of the person, I found it to be unacceptable. I did not call this person in for an interview.

This comment, by a manager in one of my classes, illustrates how important the quality of your résumé can be. This high standard also applies to your cover letter. Suggestions to make these initial documents work for you are covered separately below.

Your Résumé

The résumé is an overview of your work experience, skills, and accomplishments. You want it to speak well of you. Consider this checklist:

- **Review other résumés.** What do you like about them? Can you adapt those points for your own résumé?

- **Follow a template.** Google "résumé templates," and you will get numerous examples of ways to structure your information. Sites like myperfectresume.com will walk you through the development steps too.

- **Use effective wording.**

  - **Action verbs.** Describe your achievements by using wording like "increased sales by . . . ," "implemented a new . . . ," "cut expenses by . . . ," "reduced costs by . . . ," "grew customer base by . . . ," and so on.

  - **Keywords.** Many companies use tracking systems to look for specific qualifications. Make sure you mention the skills and requirements that the company is seeking, which are usually included in the job description.

- **Include your online presence.** Provide the links to your social media accounts. You want to demonstrate your presence and expertise in your field.

- **Add your additional experience.** Include your volunteer work, memberships, professional associations you're involved in, and any hobbies that are relevant to the position.

- **Do not lie.** Do not lie. Do not lie.

- **Have more than one résumé.** You may need different résumés for different job openings, to emphasize your experience and skills to fulfill a particular job description.

- **Proofread.** Make sure your résumé is error-free.

- **Hire a résumé writer.** If you are overwhelmed or don't have the time to create a résumé that will serve you well, you can hire a professional. Various associations offer lists of résumé writers, including The National Résumé Writers' Association and the Professional Association of Résumé Writers & Career Coaches. You can also ask your network for recommendations.

Your Cover Letter

Your cover letter is almost always sent with your résumé. It introduces you to the potential employer and explains why you would be a good fit for the position. Some of the essential points of a good letter are similar to what is required in a résumé, including tailoring the letter for the job and being error-free. Additional suggestions include:

- **Adapt a template.** You can Google "sample cover letters" and find websites with numerous templates and examples of letters—just as we discussed for résumés. You must adapt these letters to your own experience, of course. Sites such as livecareer.com will take you through the steps of creating a cover letter too.

- **Include pertinent information.** This means adding details that underscore why you are a match for the position and what benefits you will bring to the company.

- **Use a salutation.** If you don't know the person's name, address the letter to "Dear Hiring Manager" or "Dear Human Resource Representative." Remember to include your contact information.

- **Make the letter easy to read.** Use short paragraphs and vary their length. Write clearly and concisely. Use the same font you used for your résumé, and keep your comments to one page.

- **Use a professional.** Résumé writers can usually help with your cover letter, too.

Exercise

Develop an accomplishments file. When you achieve something, reach a milestone, or receive an award, mark it down or print it out and put it in a paper or computer file. When you go to update your résumé, you will have what you need to include readily available.

PRESCRIPTION FOR SUCCESS

There are some creative ways to highlight your experience, including a video résumé or a personal website that can provide more information about you than a standard résumé. Make sure these resourceful endeavors are done professionally.

73. Avoid Blunders:
Interviewing Tips for Everyone

I prepared for the interview using every bit of what we worked on together. I was very excited that they called me before I even got home to offer me the job!

You have been working on your job search, and it's beginning to pay off. You're scheduled for an interview. Now what?

There is a lot you can do to prepare for the interview, as reflected in the quote above from a senior manager I coached. The key to success is to remember that how you present yourself during the interview usually determines whether you get the job. Here are some suggestions:

Think About the Interview Ahead of Time

Who will be there? What questions will they probably ask? What strengths would you bring to the position? Check the company's website and social media sites. Know what is currently happening within the company. Your LinkedIn contacts may be able to help you identify former or current employees that you can talk to before the interview. One woman spoke to a contact who told her that the interviewer liked lots of detail. It was very helpful information, and she got the job.

Remind Yourself That It's Okay to Be Nervous

Actor Neil Patrick Harris expressed this idea before he hosted the 2015 Academy Awards, when he said, "I think, in life, being nervous about something that's forthcoming is very helpful, whether it's an awards show or a family gathering or a job interview." Let your nerves spur you to succeed. Knowing that it's okay to be a little nervous can help you stay composed and on top of your game.

Realize That the Interview Starts the Moment You Walk Out Your Door

You never know whom you may encounter on the way to the interview who could influence the outcome. There are numerous stories of people being rude to someone in traffic or the elevator, and that "someone" ends up interviewing them. One tweet said it all:

> *The man who drove into the parking space I was waiting for & told me to F-off, has arrived for his interview—WITH ME.*

Prepare for the Questions

You don't want your answers to sound memorized, but you do want to be prepared. Review the potential list of questions in Chapter 74. Know how you will answer them. Have an explanation for any gaps in your résumé, anticipate the tough questions, and do not bad-mouth your previous employer. Keep your responses positive and upbeat.

Have Stories to Tell

You may be asked to give an example of occasions when you made a good decision, overcame adversity, demonstrated leadership, and so on. You want to share a descriptive story or example that illustrates the quality the interviewer is looking for. Think about your past projects, current activities, or encounters with colleagues, bosses, friends, even strangers. What happened? What did you do? Does the story reinforce your competence? Practice telling the story using clear and concise wording. Make sure the story casts you in a good light. When I coached one young man, I asked him to describe a good decision he had made. He responded that one night when he was drinking with his buddies, he decided to become the designated driver—since he was less drunk. Not a good example!

Role-Play the Interview

Have a colleague or friend ask you questions. Become comfortable answering them and using your stories. Be open to any feedback you are given.

Choose Your Attire Carefully

You want the interviewer to listen to you, not to spend time thinking about your clothing choices. Make sure your clothes are clean and pressed. If you are told what to wear, follow those guidelines. When in doubt, you can wear a suit. Even though casual clothing may be the norm on the job, the interviewer knows you are dressing up for the interview. A colleague told me that she didn't hire someone because he dressed too casually for the interview. She felt the person didn't understand the level and importance of the new position.

Don't Forget the "Details"

Arrive 10 minutes early. Bring extra copies of your résumé. You need to be prepared in case your interviewer has misplaced the original copy or additional people come to the interview. Shake hands confidently, and with everyone in the room. Be prepared for small talk.

Portray Confidence

If you act confidently, others will perceive you that way (even if that's not how you feel). Be comfortable, but not too relaxed. Sit up straight. Look the interviewer in the eye. Don't fidget, and do not cross your arms—it will make you seem defensive.

Prepare Your Questions

Make sure you have a couple of questions ready to ask that demonstrate your interest in the position. The interviewer usually asks for such questions at the end of the interview. (See the next chapter for a guide to possible questions.)

Say Thank You

At the conclusion of the interview, say thank you, and also write thank you notes. Write to each of the people who interviewed you. An emailed note will arrive instantly. A handwritten note will stand out, but it can be late to arrive, as it may take three or four days to get to the person. Include a comment about something discussed during the interview. Send the note within 24 hours of your interview. Proof carefully.

QUESTIONS TO CONSIDER

Q. *People tell me I should negotiate salary. It looks like I'll be getting an offer soon. How do I do that?*

A. You want to be prepared to negotiate salary. Some people shy away from the conversation because it makes them uncomfortable. Yet companies often expect there to be a negotiation. You generally don't want to discuss salary until you have an offer. Before you suggest a salary range, know what is typical for the position. You can check salary surveys online, consult payscale.com and glassdoor.com, or ask a recruiter for help. If you don't ask, you won't know if an increase is possible.

You can adapt the following wording to your situation:

Everything sounds satisfactory, in fact exciting. I am wondering what can be done about the salary. It is about XX percent [or substitute the dollar amount] below what I was expecting, considering my experience with . . . .

or

Thank you. I'm delighted to receive the offer and look forward to working with your company. I believe I can contribute in a number of ways, including . . . . My concern is the salary offer. It is about XX percent below the going rate for this type of position.

Q. *I am in the process of being interviewed for a job. The person who would potentially be my supervisor has spent a considerable amount of time with me. We've even met in a* *nonofficial setting to iron out some of the concerns that I had. I want to thank him, give him a nudge about the progress of the paper work (with regard to hiring me), and at the same time keep things cordial. In this situation, would it be appropriate to text him on WhatsApp, or should I stick to email?*

A. I would email him. Since you have met in a "nonofficial setting," you want to move the conversation into the business environment. You want the supervisor to believe you are taking this potential position seriously. WhatsApp would be too informal.

PRESCRIPTION FOR SUCCESS

Don't become too casual if you know the person who is interviewing you. Be professional and answer the questions in a straightforward manner. You may be good colleagues, or even friends, but this person is now viewing you through a different lens—as a potential hire. Take the interview seriously.

74. How Do You Master Interviewing?
Practice, Practice, Practice

There is an old joke that asks, "How do you get to Carnegie Hall?" And the punch line is, "Practice, practice, practice."

The same is true for interviewing. As one person I coached said, "Once I practiced answering questions, I was no longer intimidated by interviews."

The following list of questions has been collected over the years from my seminars and my coachees' experiences. There is no one perfect way to answer, but if you know what you will say when asked these or related questions, you will be less likely to be caught off guard. Remember to include your examples or stories when you can. The last two questions provide examples of possible ways to respond. Do not copy these answers, but consider them samples of ways to answer succinctly, clearly, and positively.

Questions You May Be Asked

- What do you like best about your job/profession?
- Tell me about yourself.
- Who are your role models?
- Tell me about a time when you had to learn something very quickly.
- What are three of your weaknesses?
- Give me an example of when you demonstrated good leadership.
- What has been your biggest failure?
- Why are you interested in our company, and this job?
- Give me an example of a strategic initiative you implemented.

- What separates you from the other candidates that I will see?
- Tell me about a time when you had a dispute with a customer or colleague.
- What do you see as the major difficulties for this position?
- Tell us what inspires you.
- Say there is a scale of personality—on one end there is "tough" and on the other end there is "fair and friendly." Where are you on that scale?

  Answer: I'm everywhere on that scale. I'm tough, but fair, and I can and do develop great relationships with the people I work with. I don't think that those traits are mutually exclusive. Being tough and fair does not mean I can't be approachable and give people confidence to bring issues to my attention.

- How do you define professional success?

  Answer: I define success as being in a position where I feel challenged, where I am part of a dynamic team, and where that team is developing innovative solutions and programs to propel the organization forward. I do not define success as a title like CEO.

These questions are only a sampling. Other questions may be asked. Yet as you gain experience answering questions, you are less likely to be thrown if asked one not on this list.

Questions for You to Ask at the End of the Interview

Frequently toward the end of an interview, the interviewer will ask if you have any questions. You should have a couple ready. These questions should show your interest in the job, your potential boss, and/or the company. Adapt some of the following to your situation.

- What are the biggest challenges the person in this position will face?

- How long did the previous person hold this position?

- If I were to start tomorrow, what would you consider the top priority on my to-do list?

- What improvements or changes do you hope the new candidate will bring to this position?

- What would you consider key success factors for this job?

- What initial training is there for this position?

- Do you have any reservations about how I would fit into this organization? Do you see that I would have a role here?

Exercise

After the interview, reflect upon the questions you were asked. Did you like your answers? Would you answer differently if asked a particular question again? If so, decide how you will answer that question in a future interview.

PRESCRIPTION FOR SUCCESS

Reference your research during the interview. If asked, "Why do you want to work here?" you can mention what you saw on the company's website or one of its social media sites. It shows that you are interested in the company and that you did your homework.

75. Dress to Impress—Not to Fool the Employer

A woman wore a conservative suit to her interview, but showed up for her first day of work wearing a short leather skirt, high boots, and a number of long chains around her neck. She was sent home to change.

Another new employee wore a long-sleeve shirt and pants to his interview, but on his first day at work he wore short sleeves and shorts that revealed numerous tattoos on his arms and legs. This casual clothing was acceptable for his job, but the employee manual that he had been given clearly stated that tattoos were not to be displayed. He was sent home to change.

Both bosses of these employees told me that they felt deceived.

Prospective employees often will dress up for interviews, and then dress more casually for their daily jobs. This change is anticipated by employers, assuming professional dress is not required for a position. However, when new employees significantly alter their professional image by changing their clothing choices, how they wear their clothes, or their grooming, they are being unfair to their employers.

Such behavior also may damage a new employee's reputation. The boss could question the decision to hire that person, and doubt the new employee's professionalism. Clearly, that is not the way to start a new job.

Consider whether you are playing bait-and-switch. How would you answer the following questions? Do you think your answers would make your employer feel misled?

- Were your clothes clean and pressed for the interview, but now look like they need an iron or a visit to the cleaners?

- Are you dressing provocatively? Is your skirt significantly shorter or tighter than when you interviewed? Are you revealing cleavage?

- Were you clean-shaven at the interview, but started to grow a beard as soon as you were hired? (One executive-level man I coached told me he had done this, but he said it had set him apart from other executives, so he planned to shave.) However, if a man has a beard when he is interviewed, and gets the job, presumably it will not be a problem later.

- Are you dressing flamboyantly? Did you interview in a nondescript shirt and tie, yet show up for work in very bright-colored shirts, or ties with slogans?

PRESCRIPTION FOR SUCCESS

If you find your company's dress code too severe, try adding accessories, such as scarves, ties, or belts, to express your individuality. Remember, your job offers you many career opportunities, and dressing to fit the office requirements isn't a high price to pay for those rewards.

76. Avoid Job-Search Gaffes on Social Media

A while back, a human resources person took me aside after I presented an etiquette seminar and asked me to tell people that "asking to connect with an interviewer on LinkedIn right after an interview is considered pushy."

Her statement got me thinking. In today's world, social media is an integral part of any job search. Yet as hard as it may be for new graduates to comprehend, social media hasn't been around long enough for many people to fully understand how easy it is to make career-limiting blunders with their posts, tweets, or requests.

One obvious blunder is the misstep on LinkedIn mentioned above, where a job seeker put the interviewer in the uncomfortable position of accepting or ignoring someone who hadn't yet been hired. But it's not the only one. Here are some other mistakes to avoid when using social media during your job search:

Posting Interview Details

Keep your interview life private. Your friends only need to know that you are looking for work or have gotten a new job. If you announce on Facebook how wonderful your interview was with a particular company, you may have to announce the following week that you didn't get the job. *Ouch*. Plus, other people now know there is an opening at that company, and they may apply.

Not Keeping Your Social Media Sites Appropriate Throughout Your *Entire* Job Search

You will be checked out by prospective employers. People generally clean up their sites before they start a search, but often forget to keep them suitably professional throughout their search. It's easy to post thoughtless comments and only later realize that what you've posted isn't something you would want a prospective employer to see.

Tweeting Comments About an Interview

This mistake is similar to the first item on this list, but Twitter allows you to engage with people you know as well as those you don't know, quickly and succinctly. This can lead to ill-considered tweets like this: "I was asked, 'If you could be an animal, what would it be?' I replied, 'What sort of a stupid question is that?' Didn't get the job." This Twitter user should have considered that the comment might be seen by other prospective employers. Also, be aware that most companies monitor their Twitter feeds to see any comments made about them.

Not Looking Like Your Photograph on Any of Your Social Media Sites

It's not a good idea to feature a photo showing a many-years-younger version of yourself. (This is similar to the bait-and-switch approach in interviews discussed in the previous chapter.)

PRESCRIPTION FOR SUCCESS

Some employers will want you to have "standing" online. Depending on the job, an online presence can help present you as a thought leader in your profession. A blog can help build your personal brand. Having numerous followers reading your posts on LinkedIn or your tweets on Twitter shows your interest and influence in your field.

77. Lights, Camera, Interview!
Tips for Interviewing on Skype

On paper, the candidate looked great. But I'm really glad we spoke to him on Skype before we flew him in for an interview. He was unprepared for our questions, and messed up a number of them. We didn't fly him in, and saved a fair amount of money!

Many companies prescreen candidates via Skype before advancing to the next level of interviewing, as this comment from a human resources manager indicates. But it is not only long-distance candidates who are appearing on camera—many companies use Skype to save time as they determine whether local individuals are viable applicants. Sometimes, if it is relevant to a particular position, a Skype interview will demonstrate to an employer how a candidate will work virtually with a team.

Presenting yourself well on Skype may determine whether you move to the next step in the company's hiring process. There are two essentials to success in this area:

1. **Take the interview seriously.** Be prepared. Not only do you need to be prepared for the questions; you need to understand how to present yourself on camera.

2. **Have a practice session.** You are creating an impression as soon as the camera is turned on. Situate yourself in the same location you will use for the interview; then call a friend on Skype and have this person ask you some questions. Ask for feedback, and analyze how you appear on camera.

Before and during your interview, take note of these pointers:

- **Use a neat and uncluttered setting.** Make sure there are no controversial objects in bookshelves or on the wall behind you. Your location needs good lighting. You want to be seen clearly, without any shadows hiding your appearance. Show yourself from the waist up—not just your head.

- **Allow plenty of time before the interview to make sure the audio and video on your computer are working.** One young man didn't realize that the sound was not working on his Skype connection until his interview began. After an awkward few moments of trying to get the sound working, he had to do the interview on the phone, and he felt embarrassed throughout the conversation.

- **Create a quiet environment.** Make sure there will be no phones ringing, people walking in and out of your room, children yelling, or dogs barking during your interview.

- **Be professionally dressed.** Wear what you would wear to an in-person interview. Avoid wearing large, distracting jewelry or flashy ties.

- **Speak clearly and loudly enough to be heard.** Talk to the camera, not the image on the screen. You want to appear as if you are looking the interviewer in the eye.

- **Sit up straight.** Do not gesture too much. Don't frown. After all, you want the person to hire you.

- **Send a thank you note.** You need to thank the people who interviewed you, even if you don't get to shake their hands.

PRESCRIPTION FOR SUCCESS

Companies use other prescreening techniques besides Skype. One woman I coached was sent a list of questions and asked to record herself answering those questions. (It was a one-way interview.)

Applicants can also be screened by telephone. If you are using a cell phone, make sure it is fully charged. With a phone call, you can have notes readily available, but don't read from them. You also don't need to worry about your appearance—but you most likely will feel better if you dress as you would for an in-person interview.

78. You Got the Interview—Now Here's What to Do the Night Before

One man arrived 30 minutes late for his interview. He had programmed his GPS too quickly the night before, and had entered the street address as "Drive" instead of "Place," and it directed him to the wrong address.

Another woman was nervous the night before her interview, so she had a few drinks. She was hung over during her early interview the following morning, and responded sluggishly.

Neither of these applicants received job offers. Obviously, their candidacy was hurt by their bungling activities the night before their interviews. Don't sabotage yourself. Follow these night-before suggestions so you will shine during your job interview.

1. **Get directions to the interview site.** Be certain of the location. You don't want to get lost. Not only will your stress level increase, but you could arrive late. If driving, don't rely solely on your GPS. Double-check your route on Google maps or an app such as Waze, where drivers in your area share real-time traffic and road information. Do a dry run, if possible. Have a full tank of gas and allow time for traffic. Plan to arrive a little early.

2. **Revisit the company's website and social media sites.** You should have researched the company already, but spend just a few moments checking again. Find out if there have been any significant developments. Has the company launched a new product? Acquired a new company? Achieved a significant following on a social media site? Knowing up-to-date information demonstrates an interest in the company.

3. **Be ready for small talk.** Usually, an interview will start with some small talk, in which you should participate. You may be asked about your travel to the interview site, the weather, major sporting events, or other happenings in the world/nation/community. Be prepared to comment.

4. **Know what you will wear.** Don't wait until the morning of the interview to decide on your outfit. Try on your clothes the night before. Make sure they fit and are in good condition.

5. **Review the stories and examples that you will use when answering questions.** You should have practiced answering questions previously, but spend a little time reviewing what you plan to say. This includes the questions you may ask at the end of the interview.

6. **Have your materials ready.** Assemble extra copies of your résumé or examples of your work in a nice portfolio. Include a good pen.

7. **Have a stress-free evening.** Stay away from alcohol, and avoid quarreling with family or friends on the night before your interview. Get a good night's rest. You want to function at your best, and having enough sleep will allow you to be at the top of your game.

PRESCRIPTION FOR SUCCESS

Give yourself a pep talk. On the way to the interview, you should prepare mentally. Tell yourself positive things. I suggest saying something like, "I prepared. I can do this." Or "I'm ready. I can handle this."

79. Nice Offer ... But I Wasn't Looking for a New Job

An account executive was approached by a former colleague to join his new company.

One young woman who works for a large financial company was asked to return to a similar position in her previous department, but with more responsibility.

A sales consultant was asked to relocate to a similar position in a larger division of his company.

These individuals have what I call "good problems." *What do you do if you receive an unsolicited job offer when you are not in an active search?* How do you decide whether to accept the new position?

All three of these business professionals were happy in their current positions and had planned to stay in them for the foreseeable future. It is flattering to receive a job offer, but before you make the often-difficult decision of whether to accept a new position, you need to consider the following:

1. **Who will be your boss?** Do you know, trust, and respect this person? Does this person have your best interests at heart? Do you want to work for this person?

2. **What kind of work will you be doing?** Are you interested in doing this particular job? Will you gain new skills or valuable experience? Will this position help you to achieve your career goals? Consider your answers carefully as you decide.

3. **Will there be a significant salary increase?** Salary isn't the only consideration, but it can be an important one. Does the salary justify the risk of leaving your current position? Also, if the potential

new job involves leaving a company, your current employer may offer to match the new salary. Would this affect your decision?

4. **Are there others you can consult?** Don't go overboard, but check with a few trusted advisors and mentors. It's your decision, but they may provide valuable insights.

5. **Will there be any negative ramifications?** Will you be burning bridges? Will your current boss hold your departure against you? If so, will this matter?

6. **Why would I take this job and leave the one I already like?** Deciding to leave a job you like is not an easy choice to make. However, it could be a good career move. After answering the above questions, make a list of pros and cons for the new position. If the pros significantly outweigh the cons, seriously consider the offer.

PRESCRIPTION FOR SUCCESS

Before you accept the offer, be sure you want the job. Candidates who accept offers and then change their minds are a problem to the hiring manager. This behavior can tarnish your reputation, and it may come back to haunt you.

80. When to Let Your Employer Know You Are Leaving

I may be relocating within the next year for another job. But it might not happen. Am I being rude, for lack of a better word, by not telling my current employer? Please, let me know what you think. I need an outside opinion, not a friend's.

I am going to leave my company, as I have been accepted into graduate school overseas. Classes don't start for seven months. Should I tell my boss now?

I received these and other similar questions over the years from individuals who sought advice about quitting their jobs. They all wanted to know the same thing: Should you let your employer know that you are planning to leave your job in the somewhat distant future?

I believe very strongly in being fair to your employer, and I also believe that once you give your notice, you most likely will be marginalizing yourself within your company. You will be looked upon as the person who is "on the way out."

The general guideline is to give your employer two weeks' notice, and in many situations this is the appropriate time frame. But before you give your notice, consider the following:

1. **Adapt the standard "two weeks' notice" option for your position.** If replacing you will take your company more than two weeks, or if you need more than two weeks to train your replacement, you should provide your company sufficient time to accomplish those objectives. In some situations, however, you may encounter an unexpected response. One young man gave his two weeks' notice, but when his boss realized he was going to work for a competitor, he was told to leave immediately.

2. **No one knows what the future will hold.** By giving your notice months in advance of your departure date, you could be missing out on a promotion, a raise, or an exciting new project at your current company. These potential opportunities could change your plans.

The young man who was accepted into graduate school listened to my suggestions and decided not to tell his boss months ahead of time. A few weeks after making that decision, he unexpectedly received a very nice promotion and a raise. Consequently, he changed his plans and decided to stay at his company and attend graduate school at night.

PRESCRIPTION FOR SUCCESS

Steer clear of extreme measures when quitting. You may have seen videos that have gone viral showing people quitting their jobs by bringing in a marching band or announcing their departure by cursing out the boss on an outdoor sign. These tactics may feel good for the moment, but your future employability could be affected. Do you really think other companies would want to hire you after stunts like these?

PART V

THE FINISHING TOUCHES: YOUR ACTIONS AND APPEARANCE MAKE A DIFFERENCE

The previous sections provide numerous concrete suggestions on how to craft an effective email, make a dynamic business presentation, present yourself assertively in many types of situations, and build your career. They cover key communication essentials for success.

But you're not done yet. There is one more area to discuss.

This final section covers the "finishing touches" that will help you stand out in the crowd. These are the subtle actions that professionals use to connect with others and to encourage others to engage with them.

Your greetings, your handshake, your dining manners, your attire, your ability to make conversation, and your use of your smartphone—these things may not sound as though they are part of communicating, but they are. Done well, they help you to convey a positive impression.

By mastering these details and the others in this section, you will communicate to employees, bosses, colleagues, vendors, and clients that you are a polished businessperson.

Read on to learn the important yet straightforward steps you can take to achieve this.

81. Do You Want to Be Noticed?
The Power of Presence

When I returned to work [after a series of coaching sessions],
I received many compliments on one of my outfits. I had worn
that clothing to work 10 times in the past and no one had
complimented me about it. No one! I believe what caused this
difference was that after coaching, I was projecting myself with
confidence and making my presence known!

This comment was sent to me from a woman who had flown to New
Jersey from Jamaica for our coaching sessions, so clearly this was an
area she felt was important to her career. My reaction: What a great
story to illustrate the power of that hard-to-define something we call
presence.

What made the difference for her?

This client made a lot of changes that contributed to her success,
but the nonverbal tips ranked particularly high for her. As legendary
Hollywood heartthrob Cary Grant once observed: "It takes 500 small
details to add up to one favorable impression."

What we say and how we say it is always important. And body
language—the way our facial expressions, posture, gestures, and the
like reveal our thoughts, feelings, or intentions—also plays a large
role in how others perceive us. This has been touched on already in
some of the previous chapters, but now it is time to consider these
factors as a whole.

Being aware of the following points, and practicing them, will put
you well on the way to having positive presence.

1. **Stance.** Stand tall—you are more apt to be noticed if you do. It
   has little to do with how tall you actually are. You can stand tall
   regardless of your height. As a follower of my blog commented:

"As a petite (short!) female, I find that I have to constantly remind myself to project more 'presence' in order to be heard." Do not curve your back or pull your shoulders in; instead stand straight with your shoulders comfortably back. Avoid crossing your ankles when standing, as it makes you appear nervous. Instead, stand firmly with both feet about shoulders' width apart.

2. **Eye contact.** When you look people in the eye, they are more likely to engage with you. Many of us have a tendency to look away in an uncomfortable situation. When you do this, you tell the other person that you are nervous, which you don't want to do. Force yourself to look at the person—though you can occasionally glance away.

3. **Standard facial expression.** What is your face saying about you? Many people have what I call a "stern standard facial expression." This is what others see when you are looking at them, listening, or just not talking. (If you aren't sure what this looks like for you, look in the mirror with your neutral expression, or observe what you look like in candid photos or on video.) If you appear stern, others may choose to avoid you. You want to have a pleasant standard facial expression to let people know that you are approachable. Practice a mini smile, just enough to turn up the corners of your mouth. This gives your face a pleasant expression and conveys warmth.

4. **Gestures.** Nervous gestures can make you appear uncomfortable. Avoid wringing your hands or playing with a pen, rubber band, or any other item. These nervous mannerisms let people know that you are uneasy—which is not an image that projects powerful presence.

5. **Volume.** You can usually add power to your presence by adding appropriate volume to your voice. This is not an invitation to yell. Many people—especially women—have a tendency to speak softly. When you speak loudly enough to be heard clearly, people are less likely to ignore your ideas. Speaking too softly was a big area of concern for the businesswoman from Jamaica.

6. **Attire.** Your clothing can enhance your professional presence or detract from it. Make sure the way you dress draws attention for the right reasons—no outrageous outfits or accessories, no sloppy grooming, and no jangling jewelry.

The client from the beginning of this chapter applied each of these points, and they gave her the self-confidence she needed to enhance her presence. Others began to take note of her and her professional appearance more favorably. Within a year, she got the promotion she was seeking.

Exercise

Identify somebody within your company or network who exhibits that quality we call presence. What makes this person stand out? Are there traits you could emulate to enhance your own standing? Don't become a copycat, of course, but try to understand why this person attracts others.

PRESCRIPTION FOR SUCCESS

First impressions are important. A good first impression on a boss or client can have a major impact on your career, even if you aren't aware of it. Before meeting with a new client or possible future boss, go over the points above and make sure you are presenting the best first impression possible.

82. Do You Project Confidence When Seated?

At a meeting, a woman did not raise the seat of her chair and, as a result, sat significantly lower than the individuals on either side of her. It looked like her older siblings had brought her to the meeting.

A manager crossed her arms and perched her reading glasses on the tip of her nose. She gave the appearance of looking down at others in the meeting.

A boss leaned way back in his chair and seemed to be sleeping. His employees thought he wasn't interested in their input.

Your seated posture at meetings sends a message about you, and you want that message to be professional. This aspect of body language may seem like a little thing, but the three people profiled above all suffered negative consequences from not paying attention to how they appeared to others when seated.

Here are some suggestions for ensuring that your seated posture conveys confidence—whether you are one of twenty sitting around a large table or one of two at your yearly review with your boss.

1. **Stay still.** Don't swivel in your chair or tap your foot. Such actions become a distraction to others and can give them the impression that you are nervous. Also, don't lean way back, and never balance on just two legs of the chair. Not only does this convey the impression that you are uninterested or bored; it is potentially dangerous. If the chair tipped over, you would certainly look foolish, and you might even be injured.

2. **Adjust seat levels.** You want to be on the same level as the other members of the group, so adjust your seat height accordingly. If

this means your feet don't touch the floor, raise the chair seat as high as you comfortably can. Or as long as others cannot see, rest your feet on something under the table, such as a large dictionary or a short stool.

3. **Don't slump or look sloppy.** Sit up tall, and leave a little space between your lower back and the back of the chair. Of course, you may lean back slightly in your chair at times. Avoid folding your hands on the table (you are not in school) or crossing your arms (you appear defensive). Spread out, but don't encroach on someone else's space. In her book *Lean In*, Sheryl Sandberg referenced a posture study in the professional journal *Psychological Science*:

> *When people assumed a high-power pose (for example, taking up space by spreading their limbs) for just two minutes, their dominance hormone levels (testosterone) went up and their stress hormone levels (cortisol) went down. As a result, they felt more powerful and in charge and showed a greater tolerance for risk. A simple change in posture led to a significant change in attitude.*

4. **Pay attention to your lower half.** Depending on the type of table at which you are seated, your legs may be visible to others. Keep both feet on the floor, although you may cross your ankles. Try not to cross your legs—it's bad for your circulation, among other things.

   Pay attention to your clothing, too. One man I worked with wore black slacks, black shoes, and white socks, which were noticeable when he crossed one knee over the other. Women who wear short skirts need to be aware that when they sit, those skirts will hike up and expose a lot of leg.

5. **Make sure you take a seat** *at* **the table.** Do not sit on one of those chairs that are often arranged against the wall. Arrive early enough to get a seat at the table. You want to be part of the discussion, not an observer. If a shortage of seats at the table is a chronic problem, you may have no choice but to sit against the wall on occasion. Don't let this silence you. Speak up if you have an opinion or

suggestion to offer. If appropriate, stand to speak so everyone is aware of your presence.

PRESCRIPTION FOR SUCCESS

Learn to communicate in your discomfort zone. Sometimes you can do little to control the conditions at a meeting, but identifying the cause of your discomfort is half the battle toward overcoming it. For instance, it you cannot adjust the seat height, sit up as straight as you can and project self-confidence. You may not feel it, but your colleagues won't know that.

83. Greetings: The Power of a Simple "Hello"

When I encountered a guest waiting for the elevator in the casino where I work as a bartender, I made sure to say "Hello," and then we had a pleasant conversation as we rode the elevator together. Later that night, this same man happened to stop by my bar for a drink. I greeted him again, and he remembered me and how friendly I was to him. Apparently he had enjoyed a lucky night and won a lot of money. When he was leaving, he tipped me with a black chip! ($100) I was definitely happy that I had said "Hello."

Sometimes it literally pays to be friendly, as one of my undergraduate students learned during his part-time job tending bar at a local casino.

Regardless of where you work, however, there are lots of benefits to greeting people. These include making your presence known, establishing a basic connection with colleagues and customers, helping others to feel comfortable, and creating a more pleasant and welcoming work environment.

Yet this powerful—and simple—act of acknowledging someone is often neglected.

People often believe that they greet others, but when observed, they actually don't. Others don't greet people because they are shy, they are preoccupied, or they don't realize they should. Yet most people want to be part of a friendly workplace. Check your behavior against these basic greeting guidelines:

1. **Greet people you *don't* know as well as those you do.** Let me stress this—you don't need to know people to say "Hello." I am not talking about strangers on a dark street, but I am suggesting that you greet people where you work during your daily interac-

tions with them. The old saying, "Don't talk to strangers," doesn't apply to the workplace! Not all greetings are equal, however. Some people use "Hey." This is a very casual greeting, and usually not recommended for corporate use. As for the even more casual, sloppy greeting "Yo!"—don't use it.

2. **If someone says "Hello" to you, you must respond.** It is rude not to acknowledge this basic courtesy. One woman in a corporate etiquette class said that she was going to stop greeting people because many of them didn't respond. Another participant quickly spoke up. "Oh, please don't," she said. "When I was new here you always greeted me, and it made me feel comfortable." Yet, she admitted that she didn't know to acknowledge the greetings. After this exchange, she vowed to do so in the future.

   Usually, it's not malice that causes people not to respond— it's ignorance of this practice. A woman in one of my seminars said "Hello" to a security guard every night as she left work. He *never* responded. Yet when a friend of the woman asked the guard whether he knew her, he said, "Oh, yes, I know her. She says 'Hello' to me every night. She's great."

3. **Remember that "How are you?" is not a question when used as part of the greeting.** If someone says "Hi. How are you," do not answer with any description of your ailments. This nonquestion is simply a polite convention. The only response should be, "Fine. How are you?" or "I'm well, thanks. How are you?"

QUESTION TO CONSIDER

Q. *Do I have to keep greeting the same people if I see them numerous times during the workday? I hope not.*

A. You don't. But you do need to acknowledge them with a smile or a nod of the head.

PRESCRIPTION FOR SUCCESS

Monitor your greeting behavior over the next two weeks. Do you greet people? Many are surprised at the results of this exercise. One woman was certain that she greeted people, but after doing this exercise, she realized that she only greeted people she knew. As she said: "Who knew! I could have sworn I greeted everyone."

84. Introductions: Frustrations Galore!

Silence. I get a lot of silence after I introduce myself to people. Shouldn't people respond with their names?

Yes, they should.

But it seems that a lot of people don't know how to respond to an introduction, judging from how often in my classes I am asked variations on the question above.

It can be frustrating for people when others don't reply to this straightforward attempt to connect. One woman told me that when people don't say anything, she is forced to ask, "And you are?" But she added, "I think that can sometimes sound harsh." I assured her that she was reacting correctly—as long as there was no critical tone in her words.

I believe that people stay silent because they don't know what to say, they are caught off guard, or they are shy. Yet it is important for people to say something and eliminate that awkward silence.

Follow these three suggestions to respond appropriately:

1. **Use a greeting.** Say "Hi" or "Hello" before you introduce yourself. It is more pleasant when you do. Make sure you are looking at the person as you speak.

2. **Respond with your full name.** When people do respond, some give just their first names. You should say both your first and last names. This will help people remember you, and also differentiate you from any other colleague with the same first name. You also can personalize your response (and help yourself remember the other person's name) by repeating that name, too, such as "Hi, Chris, I'm Cara Smith," or "Hello, Mr. Jones, I'm Jennifer Cortez." Speak slowly so people understand what you are saying.

3. **Add a "welcoming statement."** After you give your name, add a
   little something. This will help encourage conversation. For example, you might say, "Nice to meet you. I heard that you had
   just joined us from ABC Company."

PRESCRIPTION FOR SUCCESS

If you forget the name of someone you have to introduce, just admit it. You can say, "I've
forgotten your name. Please excuse me" or "I'm sorry. I'm blanking on your name."

85. Not for Men Only!
The Etiquette of the Handshake

When did women start shaking hands? It feels awkward.

A very bright, talented professional woman asked me that question. Initially, I was startled. Yet as I thought about the question, I realized that many women in my seminars are reluctant to shake hands, and others do so incorrectly.

In today's workplace, shaking hands is not for men only. The handshake is the business greeting: Both men and women need to shake hands, and to do so correctly.

One woman told me she got her job because she shook hands at the beginning of the interview and again at the end. The manager told the woman that he chose her because she handled herself so professionally. Another woman realized that she had been the only one at her table who stood when she shook hands with her CEO. As a result, she had a conversation with him; the other individuals did not.

Why do women sometimes feel uncomfortable about shaking hands? The reasons vary:

1. **Some women were never taught to shake hands.** It is not that these women were *told* not to do so; it is that they were not *taught* to do so. One woman in an etiquette class was shocked when she realized that she was not teaching her four-year-old daughter to shake hands, but she had already started teaching her two-year-old son to shake hands.

2. **Women bring the personal greeting of kissing friends on the cheek into the workplace.** This can be awkward, since you will not want to kiss or hug everyone you meet at work, nor will everyone be comfortable with that greeting.

3. **Many women were taught that they did not need to stand when shaking hands.** Before each of my seminars, I walk around the room to introduce myself to my participants and extend my hand in a greeting. Approximately 70 to 75 percent of men, but only 25 to 30 percent of women, stand to shake my hand. You establish your presence when you stand. Both men and women should stand when shaking hands.

You will be judged by your handshake. To shake hands properly:

- Extend your hand with the thumb up.

- Touch thumb joint to thumb joint with the person you are greeting. Put your thumb down, and wrap your fingers around the palm of the other person.

- Make sure your grip is firm, but not enough to bruise the other person.

- Don't overshake. Two to three pumps is enough. Face the person and make eye contact.

And one more thing: It used to be that men needed to wait for a woman to extend her hand. Not anymore. The current guideline is to give the higher-ranking person a split second to extend his or her hand, and if he or she does not, you extend yours. The key is that the handshake needs to take place.

QUESTION TO CONSIDER

Q. It's flu season; do I still need to shake hands?

A. I understand the concern, but you will be excluding yourself if you don't participate in this business ritual. Keep wipes handy and subtly clean your hand afterward. Also remember to sneeze into your *left* elbow. This way your right hand stays clean.

PRESCRIPTION FOR SUCCESS

To eliminate an unwanted hug, put out your hand to initiate the handshake as soon as you see the hugger approaching you. You will be establishing the mode of greeting. This proactive behavior will eliminate a lot of unwelcome hugging.

86. Cubicle Conversations: Keep Chat Professional in the Office

I can't believe she was discussing her sex life. Ugh. I didn't need to hear it.

Small talk with colleagues allows you to get to know them, and them to get to know you. This can create a bond that can help you work together more efficiently and productively. It also helps establish a more pleasant work environment. But there are guidelines. As the woman quoted above underscored in one of my classes, certain topics are off-limits.

Yet it is important to engage in small talk. If you don't, your colleagues may think that you are a snob, or perhaps that you have something to hide. Either way, this can lead to speculation and gossip, which could prove detrimental to your career—and your reputation.

And please don't tell me, as many people do, that small talk isn't your thing. If you follow these guidelines, you will be able to chat casually with the best of them.

1. **Share a little.** You need to reveal a little about yourself to have things to discuss. You don't want to disclose all the details, but letting people know a little about your life—for instance, your hobbies, that you like classical music, or that your children play lacrosse—can help you find common areas for discussion.

2. **Give the person your undivided attention.** Demonstrate interest in the person you're talking to by looking at him or her and listening—don't look at your phone, watch other people, or text. And don't interrupt. It's annoying to others to have a conversation with someone who constantly interrupts them. If you must take a call during the conversation, let the person know why, such as: "I am waiting to hear from my colleague about a deadline change."

3. **Choose conversation topics judiciously.** Stay away from controversial areas, especially the often-mentioned "big three": Sex, politics, and religion. People can have very strong opinions about these issues, and may want to engage you in conversation about them. Resist the temptation—it's too easy to say something that offends your customer or colleague, and arguments may develop. Other topics to avoid, except with very close friends: Your health (no one wants to hear about your hernia operation) and your wealth (how much you spend on your clothes, jewelry, vacation, car, and so on is nobody else's concern).

   Good topics to discuss include movies, television shows, holiday plans, vacations, the event or seminar you are attending, upbeat business news, noncontroversial current events, professional achievements of others, sporting events, and the weather (assuming it's somewhat out of the ordinary).

4. **Use LinkedIn to gain information.** This is neither stalking nor an invasion of privacy, but simple preparation. If you are meeting with people you don't know, look them up. You may find areas of interest. Did you attend the same school? Work for the same companies? You can mention in conversation that you noticed this information on the person's profile.

5. **Don't become "Negative Ned."** This is the person who continually brings up negative topics, such as the war in Afghanistan, how bad the economy is, or what a sad state the world is in. People will avoid you if you are always a downer. They also avoid complainers, people who never have a nice word to say about anything but find plenty to complain about.

6. **Ask questions,** especially open-ended questions that usually result in more expansive answers that can lead to conversations. These could include such queries as "What's your background?" or "How did you get involved in the project?" A closed-ended question frequently elicits just a one-word answer, such as yes or no. Instead of asking "Did you enjoy the conference?"—to which the answer

may be a simple "Yes, thanks"—try something like "What did you learn from the workshop on . . . ?" instead.

QUESTION TO CONSIDER

Q. *Is it appropriate to start a conversation with "May I make a suggestion?"*

A. I would not start a conversation with "May I make a suggestion?" Offering suggestions needs to evolve from a discussion with others. And even then, I would be more likely to say, "I have some suggestions. Are you interested?"

PRESCRIPTION FOR SUCCESS

Be up-to-date with your profession. It's hard to discuss developments in your field if you aren't familiar with them. Read your professional journals and magazines. It's easy to strike up a conversation with a colleague by saying something like, "Did you see the article in *XYZ* magazine about Max Smith's research? That process could be helpful for us." Even if your colleague hasn't read the article, it allows you to develop a conversation by telling him or her a little about it.

87. Effective International Communication: You Say "Potato," and I Say . . .

I told an international seminar participant that some guidelines weren't "carved in stone." He looked perplexed and said, "I didn't see that stone."

Today's workplace is global, and many employees and entrepreneurs are working with colleagues and customers all over the world. Being sensitive to cultural differences can enhance your working relationships and stop you from making potentially costly and often embarrassing mistakes.

The above anecdote illustrates the pitfalls of using idiomatic expressions with people from other countries. And when I tell that story in the United States, my students laugh, but it helps them to grasp the intricacies and difficulties of communicating internationally.

Listed below are some pointers to help you communicate professionally when working overseas, or with international colleagues in the United States.

1. **Learn about other cultures.** The more you know about other cultures, the easier it is to adapt to the differences. The Internet makes this easy. If you Google "etiquette" and the name of the country or region in which you are interested, you will find more information than you can possibly use. There are also culture-specific guidebooks available. When I was scheduled to coach a businesswoman in China, I wanted to know whether wearing a red jacket for our first session would be appropriate. I knew colors were important in China, so I checked the Internet and discovered that red represents happiness and good fortune. I wore the jacket.

2. **Don't criticize someone else's manners.** What you consider bad manners may be the acceptable way of doing something in a dif-

ferent culture. In the United States, making noise when eating is considered bad manners. Yet in some cultures, such as Japan, it is showing appreciation for the food.

3. **It is the visitor who must adapt.** This is the standard rule of international etiquette. That familiar adage, "When in Rome, do as the Romans do," is absolutely true. If you are the visitor, you need to alter your style to be in sync with your host and your international location. And be respectful of the differences you encounter. It's unrealistic to expect your host to change for you—though a very gracious host will meet you more than halfway. A woman in Australia that I coached via Skype wanted to meet on her lunch hour. This meant I would have to call her at eight or nine o'clock at night—late by my working standards. I adjusted my schedule.

4. **Don't yell—just speak more slowly!** When working internationally, you will encounter people who are speaking English as their second or third language. If a person doesn't understand your comments, it doesn't mean that he or she is deaf, so it won't help to raise your voice and repeat what you said. The person simply may need more time to process the language.

5. **Avoid using buzzwords.** In the United States, we use phrases in business that can be difficult for others to comprehend if English isn't their native tongue. Think about the literal meanings of such phrases as *ballpark figure* or *push the envelope*—do they make any sense in connection with business? Of course not! Now imagine how incomprehensible such terms become when translated into another language.

6. **Be aware that American English is different from British English.** Some words have different meanings from one English-speaking country to another. In the United States, a truck is a *truck*, but it's a *lorry* in Britain. And *two weeks* is a *fortnight*, a car's *trunk* is a *boot*, an *elevator* is a *lift*, *sneakers* are *trainers*, and so on. There are also differences in spelling (*center* or *centre*, *check* or *cheque*) that matter when communicating in writing. Generally

speaking, use your native version of English, but be aware that your correspondent is doing the same.

7. **Learn the differences in nonverbal communication.** Two important areas are eye contact and hand gestures. In some cultures, it is a sign of respect to avert the eyes when conversing with someone. In the United States, however, we stress direct eye contact during conversations, and if someone isn't looking at us, we assume that person is not listening. Also, gestures have different meanings depending where you are in the world. The classic American "thumbs-up" sign of approval translates as a vulgarity in some cultures. When you are aware of differences like these, you are less likely to make negative and possibly erroneous assumptions about people from other countries.

8. **Know the variations in business-card exchanges.** In Japan, for example, it is customary to exchange cards before conversation begins. It's part of the initial greeting: You greet the person, bow, and present your card to your host with two hands. This means you are giving the card with full measure. In the Middle East, business cards are exchanged with the right hand only. The left hand is considered dirty, so it would be improper to touch the business card with it. If you are traveling to another country on business or doing business with international people in the United States, check online for the appropriate protocols.

9. **Be cautious with humor.** Avoid telling jokes in conversation, as humor doesn't travel well. As a former teacher of English as a second language, I know that you need to be really fluent in a language to be able to joke successfully in that language. A Chinese friend told me it took her eight years to understand the American sense of humor!

PRESCRIPTION FOR SUCCESS

Always assume someone will understand your words, even if you are surrounded by people who purportedly don't speak your language.

When I was teaching a class in the Middle East, there was some side conversation in Arabic during the class. From the participants' body language, I knew that the discussion was about me. Eventually, I stopped teaching and said:

"You know that I have only spoken English in this class." My students nodded.

"You also know that I am American." They nodded again.

"But don't I look a little Middle Eastern, with my dark hair, big eyes, and olive complexion?" They nodded, but apprehensively this time.

"You are assuming that I don't understand your language . . . but you may be very wrong." They stopped nodding, but the look of fear on their faces as they thought I had understood their side conversations was priceless.

I continued teaching, and I didn't tell them that I didn't understand Arabic until later in the day. But there were no more side conversations!

88. Ways to Engage with People—for People Who Don't Like to Engage!

My customer complained to my supervisor that I answered the phone, "Yeah. What's up?"

I was told that if I wanted to move up in my organization, I had to get out of my office more.

How could she not know what an Ethernet cord is? When I finally said "the blue cord," she got it!

Lately, I have worked with a number of people with outstanding technical skills whose career growth has been limited by their inability to connect with others. They were referred to me for coaching to provide them with the necessary skills to engage successfully with coworkers, bosses, customers, and clients.

People want to hire, work with, promote, and do business with others whom they know and like. If you were not born with the "gift of gab," and many people weren't, you can learn the skills that enable you to connect with others. Here are some suggestions that will help you to engage more easily:

1. **Be approachable.** Some people have told me that they don't want to be approached because people will ask them work questions. My response is twofold: You don't have to answer every question asked of you. You can use a polite line to defer your response, such as, "I'm on my way to a meeting; please call or text me to schedule some time." But if the question has a simple answer, why not help the person immediately? Chances are, he or she will find you later anyway.

2. **Keep your phone off the table when meeting with someone.** Yes, you read that correctly. Having your phone visible tells the other person, "I am *so* ready to drop you and connect with someone else." And some people put two phones on the table!

3. **Do your homework.** Knowing a little about topics that are important to your customers and colleagues will make it easier to make conversation. You don't have to be an expert on every topic, but learn enough to allow you to participate. And convey interest in the person through your body language. Look at him or her, and maintain a pleasant facial expression.

4. **Don't overload people with unnecessary information.** Only give them as much data as *they* need. Some technical people believe that they have to impart all the facts, but their customers, colleagues, or bosses may have a lower threshold for details—and tune out once it is reached.

5. **Remember "the blue cord."** You should use language that your colleagues or customers will understand. Using a technical word that someone doesn't recognize can distance you from that person. Some people understand what to do if they are told to "pull out the Ethernet cord" from amid a tangle of cables, but those who are less tech-savvy need simpler terms: "Pull out the blue cord."

6. **Learn to socialize.** This is an important business skill. You get to meet people, and they get to meet *you*, which can benefit you in many ways. You may meet potential new customers, enhance your chances of promotion, or simply enjoy some new friends. Go up to people, greet them, shake hands, and make conversation. The more you do it, the easier it will get.

7. **Call people.** Don't communicate via email and text exclusively. Calling people on the phone when appropriate creates a more personal connection. Also remember to sound pleasant and enthusiastic. When you answer the phone, be friendly. Say hello, give your name ("Gavin Jones speaking"), and, when appropriate, ask, "How may I help you?"

8. **Don't ignore pen and paper.** If a colleague or client comes to your office for a meeting, avoid taking notes on your laptop. Not only does taking notes in this manner draw your attention away from the other person, but the raised computer screen becomes a barrier between the two of you. An iPad or other tablet is okay. But taking any necessary notes the old-school way—with pen and paper—can be just as efficient and less intrusive.

PRESCRIPTION FOR SUCCESS

These are not the only ways to engage with others, but they are important ones. As you go through your day, remind yourself of the value of connecting and make a conscious effort to reach out. Soon these actions will become second nature to you.

89. The "Halo Effect"—
When Being Nice Has Benefits

I had the following conversation with my son after he had his car serviced:

Mom, they did a great job on my car.

Why do you say that?

As I was leaving, we talked about new cars, and the mechanic told me to have a safe trip home.

Jake knows very little about the inner workings of cars, but because the mechanic was nice and friendly to him, Jake believed that the man had done a good job on his vehicle.

He is not alone in how he judges the quality of someone's work.

A colleague recently decided to place an order with one software vendor over another because, as she said, "He was so friendly." She had spoken to a number of people, but said that the one she chose was the easiest to talk to.

Another example comes from one of my students, who raved to her colleagues about a fast-food restaurant. They responded with their comments on other restaurants. She realized after a few moments that they weren't talking about the food—only about their experiences as customers. They all commented that when servers, cashiers, hostesses, and so on were pleasant, the students would return to the restaurants. If the staffers weren't friendly, the students went elsewhere for food. (And remember, they were discussing fast-food restaurants!)

I call this phenomenon the "halo effect" of being nice. (The term "halo effect" was first coined in 1920 by psychologist Edward Thorndike, who concluded that your impression of someone will influence your view of his or her abilities.)

One of my clients summed it up best when she said: "The service you give people will affect their perception of the quality of your work." But before you jump to any conclusions, I am not saying that the quality of your work doesn't matter. It does.

Being nice and friendly will not make up for inferior work. What it will do is encourage people to view you and your work positively. People will enjoy working with you or for you if you are nice to them. And that is an advantage in everyone's line of work.

There are actions you can take that encourage people to react to you in a positive way. Two that already have been discussed in this section are greeting people and engaging in small talk with them. Other positive actions include:

Offering to Help, When You Can

If someone (male or female) is struggling with packages, or seems overloaded with assignments, assisting that person is a nice thing to do—without expecting anything in return. But it is very likely that when you help someone, he or she will remember it and help you or someone else in the future.

Giving Compliments

Give sincere compliments to colleagues and customers when appropriate. Provide some specifics, if possible, such as, "You were well-prepared for the questions after your presentation, and it emphasized how knowledgeable you are on this topic." But be careful not to cross any professional or sexist lines—it's not appropriate for a man to tell a woman that she looks cute or sexy in a particular outfit or for a woman to compliment a man on his buff biceps.

Having an Exit Line

An exit line establishes the ending of the encounter and paves the way for the next meeting. Sample exit lines include "Nice talking to you,"

"Have a great weekend," or "Have a safe trip home." I recently went to the doctor for a minor concern, and he had a great exit line that I have added to my list of favorites. As he was ending our visit, he added, "If it happens again, I'm here for you." (This isn't suitable for every occasion, of course, but it is a warmly affirming line for an appropriate encounter, such as addressing a colleague's minor problem.)

PRESCRIPTION FOR SUCCESS

Good, friendly customer service is always a plus. But what of the reverse? Be fair. If you have a problem with the service or some other aspect of a business transaction, ask to speak to the manager. Before you go public and post your comments on the Internet, give the organization a chance to make things right.

90. "But It's Playing My Song": Smart Phone Use for Business

In a *New York Times* article, "Pass the Word: The Phone Call Is Back," reporter Jenna Wortham wrote that her friends had started "picking up their cellphones for an unusual purpose: They wanted to talk. And I started answering when they called."

Her article highlights that the need for vocal contact is still alive and well. And for some of us, of course, the phone call never went away.

Talking to someone on the phone is still an important way to communicate in business—you can get immediate feedback or acknowledgment, you can eliminate the back-and-forth aspects of texts or emails, and the way you use your voice can enhance or clarify your message.

You also can have more in-depth discussions. My executive-level niece always calls me when she needs to discuss her next career move, because she wants a fair amount of interaction and advice.

Here are some suggestions for using smartphones smartly in business:

1. **Answer the phone professionally.** The smartphone allows you to conduct your business from almost anywhere. You should answer calls in a manner that gives the impression you are at work (whether you are working from the office or Starbucks!). Use a greeting—"Hello" or "Good morning"—and give your full name when answering the phone—"Good morning. Roberto Jackson speaking." (Of course, if you know from caller ID that it is your colleague, you can simply say "Hi, Jen.")

2. **Meetings trump phones.** Since the smartphone has become so much a part of people's lives, the phone is always "at the ready," and people can answer it at inappropriate times—such as dur-

ing meetings. You want to give your undivided attention to the person with whom you are meeting. Also, as we've mentioned elsewhere in this section, don't place your phone on the table. It gives the impression that you are ready to answer it at the first ring. Research has shown that the presence of a phone inhibits face-to-face conversation.

3. **Keep your ears unencumbered.** Put your earbuds away, and don't use a Bluetooth headset in the office—even if it is disguised as a necklace or some other accessory—when interacting with others. Even if the listening devices aren't in your ears, it looks as though you are ready to reconnect at any moment. It's off-putting. You want your colleagues or customers to see you as ready to engage with *them*. (You can use your earbuds to listen to music if you are alone.)

4. **Check your voice mail.** Many people don't leave messages when making personal calls. They know that people will see that they called, and call them back. In business, people still leave messages, and you should be sure to listen to yours promptly. If you are the one leaving a message, give the reason for the call, and make your points in as few words as necessary because people are likely to stop listening if you ramble.

5. **Don't speak too loudly.** You don't want to disturb others when you are talking on the phone. Also, you don't want others to overhear business information that may be confidential or of a sensitive nature. Speak clearly in a quiet, conversational voice.

6. **Do not make excuses for your errors.** When sending emails from their smartphones, some people add a generic message at the end, such as: "Please excuse typos and the brevity of this message. Sent from my mobile device." Mentioning possible errors not only highlights any you may have made, but also indicates that you couldn't be bothered checking and correcting. Take the time to proof and correct your messages before you send them.

PRESCRIPTION FOR SUCCESS

Use or create a ring tone that doesn't startle or scare people. You don't want your colleagues or business associates to be shocked when your phone rings.

91. The Etiquette of Connecting Professionally on LinkedIn

Should I be on LinkedIn? I am already on Facebook, Instagram, and Twitter.

Many of my students and business professionals have asked this question, and my answer is always yes. But I have coached numerous professionals who were not on LinkedIn, or who had incomplete profiles, used fuzzy photos of themselves, and had typos on their write-ups.

LinkedIn is *the* social network for professionals to connect and network with other businesspeople. According to Wikipedia, LinkedIn has well over 433 million members. That's a lot of people with whom you might network!

There are, of course, other platforms, including Facebook and Twitter, which entrepreneurs and companies use to promote themselves or their businesses. But whether you are new to the workplace or a seasoned pro, it is important that you have an individual presence on LinkedIn and understand the etiquette of connecting. (As a business owner, I have an individual LinkedIn profile for Barbara Pachter as well as a business Facebook page, www.facebook.com/pachtertraining.)

Here are some suggestions:

When You Ask Others to Connect with You

1. **Make sure your profile is complete and up-to-date.** People will look you up to refresh their memories of who you are. Your profile can include more information than your résumé. Take advantage of this opportunity to list your awards, interests, courses taken, or anything else that enhances your image. And make sure there are no typographical errors in your profile. You are creating your brand.

2. **Include a professional headshot.** Your photograph should look like you. You want the image to be in focus and to have a clear background. Wear appropriate work attire. You should be looking at the camera. According to LinkedIn, profiles with a photo get 14 times more views than those without one.

3. **Invite people you are acquainted with to connect with you.** Linke-dIn suggests that you "Only invite people you know well and who know you." Try to get 500 connections. That's the highest number of connections listed on a LinkedIn profile. Achieving that level lends some credibility to your standing in your profession. If you are new to the workplace, that number may seem hard to accomplish initially. Yet working toward 500 can keep you focused on building your network.

4. **Customize your request.** Avoid using the default request message ("I'd like to add you to my professional network on LinkedIn"), and personalize your comments. Remind the person how you know each other. You can mention someone you know in common, how you value the person's expertise, or the reason you want to connect. Use the person's profile page to connect. If you just click on "People You May Know," you are not able to personalize the request.

5. **Don't repeat your request.** This can become annoying. LinkedIn will remind people of your request, so you don't need to send another message.

When Others Ask You to Connect

1. **Have a strategy for accepting people.** Once you accept someone's invitation, that person will have access to people you know, and may ask you about them. Also, you will get updates on the new connection's activities. Some people accept everyone to build their numbers; others follow LinkedIn's suggestion and accept only those they know well.

2. **Know how to respond to a request.** The main options are to *accept* or *ignore*. If you click the *ignore* option, you can also (a) report the

invitation as spam or (b) select "I don't know this person." These choices provide feedback to LinkedIn on whether to restrict the sender's account, so choose these options carefully.

3. **Respond promptly.** Accept invitations quickly. Otherwise, the person may think you are debating whether to connect. Or the person may think that you don't remember who he or she is.

Once You Are Connected

1. **Keep your profile updated.** Add any new responsibilities, promotions, or new jobs. Add relevant videos or PowerPoint presentations that feature you or your work. It is also fine to add certifications or achievements not related to your current career, if they enhance your professionalism. These will help you to stand out from the crowd.

2. **Disable your notifications for minor updating.** This is especially important if your boss is part of your network, as updating can make it appear that you are job-searching. Also, this way your network isn't notified every time you add routine information to your profile.

3. **Stay in touch with your network.** Now that you have connections, politely develop the relationship. Respond promptly to messages. Endorse people you have worked with, and write recommendations when appropriate. Leave positive comments on your connections' updates, especially when they announce a new job or promotion.

PRESCRIPTION FOR SUCCESS

Use the Help Center. There is a lot to know about using LinkedIn. For instance, under Settings and Accounts, you can access the Help Center. It covers additional ways to build your profile, grow your network, and apply for jobs. Keep in mind that LinkedIn, like other social media, is always evolving.

92. We Can't All Be Steve Jobs: Dressing Well Reaps Results

I'm being considered for promotion and need to know how to dress so people see me as a manager.

I was one of four rough-and-tumble boys. We didn't care about clothes growing up. I'm just starting out in the workplace—what do I do?

Many people have concerns about looking professional when dressing for work, as the above comments from some of my students indicate. This can be a challenging question to answer since what constitutes "business casual" is not always easily defined.

The key to dressing well in any working environment is to think about your attire. This may sound strange to you, but give some attention to your clothing choices. Your clothing sends a message about you, and you want to be in control of that message.

What do your clothes say about you? Do they project professionalism?

One boss said to his employee, "I gave you the new project because I trust that you will always show up professionally dressed for our meetings."

Steve Jobs, the late founder of Apple, wore a black turtleneck and jeans. Facebook's Mark Zuckerberg wears grey T-shirts. And nobody could argue that these men haven't done well. But as the title of this chapter says, we cannot all be Steve Jobs. Most of us need to dress well to do well.

I have coached numerous people on appropriate dressing for work. Here are some suggestions to guide your clothing choices:

1. **Ask yourself: Does my company have a dress code?** Know what your company allows and doesn't allow, and make sure your attire

fits the guidelines. Some organizations allow jeans; others do not. If the guidelines aren't clearly defined, ask someone who knows.

2. **Know what's appropriate for your company.** Notice what other employees wear to work. High-tech firms may be very casual, yet financial firms may still be formal. Large companies may be more conservative than smaller ones. Appropriate work attire may also differ depending on where your company is located—consider New York City vs. Albuquerque.

3. **Think about your schedule when choosing your clothes.** Will you be interacting with clients or potential clients, presenting at a conference, or meeting with the higher-ups? Will you need to change your typical work attire for these activities? One man said that his company is very casual about dress, but his clients are more formal. He always wears a suit when going to their offices. Another man said that he works for a social media start-up and doesn't tuck in his shirt when working in his office, but he always tucks it in when going to a client's office.

4. **Know what is appropriate for your next position.** As you move up—or aspire to move up—in an organization, you may need to upgrade your attire. I was hired to coach a new executive who was going to be working overseas, and his bosses felt he needed to upgrade his wardrobe to present a more professional image internationally. Observe what higher-ranked employees wear. Usually, you can model your clothing choices on their style of dress. You also can ask a trusted mentor for guidance.

5. **Buy good-quality, classic items.** They are made better and fit better. You may spend more money on each item, but your clothes will last longer. If you buy trendy outfits, they will go out of style quickly. If you buy timeless essentials, they will last multiple seasons and ultimately save you money.

6. **Pay attention to your accessories.** You want to wear good-quality accessories. Worn wisely, they can add color and style to your attire. Plus, they can be an easy way to update your clothing to

make you appear current with any fashion trends. But you do not want them to overpower you or your clothing. Don't be like the supervisor who wore numerous rings, bracelets, and necklaces all at one time! And remember that people will notice what's on your wrist. A good watch still stands out as a classy accessory, and a Fitbit can tell people you are concerned about your health.

7. **Don't ignore your grooming.** Even though your clothing is casual, you want people to focus on your abilities—not on distracting details. You do not want people noticing dandruff on your shirt, smudges on your glasses, or lipstick on your teeth. Make sure your breath is odor-free, and limit or eliminate perfume and cologne. Many people are allergic. Check for missing buttons, hanging threads, and scuffed shoes. Do not have chipped nail polish or nose hairs that need to be clipped. They become distractions.

8. **When in doubt, leave it out.** If you are unsure whether something is appropriate, don't wear it. Choose something that you know will be okay.

PRESCRIPTION FOR SUCCESS

Learn about clothes. Read books or articles online about business clothing. Establish a relationship with a good salesperson in a quality store. He or she will know what you are looking for and often put those items aside for you. Use a professional shopper. Sign up for emails from your favorite stores. They will let you know about sales and offer other information on clothing.

93. Top 10 Business Clothing Mistakes

She showed a lot of cleavage. I didn't know where to look.

I didn't remember his name. I referred to him as "the man in the red pants."

She looked like she just rolled out of bed—her clothes were wrinkled and her hair was wet.

I am often asked about what professionals should wear to work. The questions—from bosses, employees, and even reporters—focus on how employees should dress in today's casual workplace, indicating that years after the "rules" were relaxed, many are still confused and dressing inappropriately.

The key point I always stress, whether I am discussing a young man getting ready to interview for his first job or a senior director courting a new client, is that you don't want your clothing choices to undermine your credibility, as the comments above indicate can happen.

My list of the Top 10 Business Clothing Mistakes is based on what I have seen in the workplace as well as suggestions from my seminar participants. It focuses on what you should *not* do:

1. **Do not disregard suggestions when told what to wear.** If a recruiter tells you to wear a suit to the interview, wear a suit. If your client tells you to stop wearing a suit, stop wearing a suit! One young business owner didn't hire someone because the potential employee kept coming to the interviews in a business suit, when he was told not to do so. If you don't follow instructions about your clothing, why would a potential employer think you would follow instructions if you worked together?

2. **Do not dress in clothes that do not fit.** If your clothes are too big, you look like a little kid in your big brother's or sister's clothing.

If your clothing is too tight, you could be flaunting your body. Both men and women need to use a good tailor and make sure their clothes fit properly.

3. **Do not look like you just got out of bed.** Casual dress does not mean sloppy. Your hair needs to be clean and styled, and your clothing needs to be clean and pressed. No holes. No frays. One woman I know of doesn't dry her hair or put on her makeup until she is at work. This ignores the facts that people see her entering the workplace and her colleagues are annoyed she is using work time to finish getting dressed.

4. **Do not wear skirts that are too short.** Short skirts draw attention to your legs and expose you to ogling. Plus, you may find yourself labeled with a trivializing nickname. Would you like to be known as "Lana Legs"? Also, make sure your underwear—including bra straps—does not show.

5. **Do not wear short socks.** Short socks, or socks that fall down, expose skin and hairy legs on men when they sit and/or cross their legs. It is distracting, and not an attractive look.

6. **Do not show cleavage.** If you wear low-cut tops that expose cleavage, you draw attention to this body part and emphasize your sexuality. Is this what you want to be remembered for?

7. **Do not draw attention to your clothing because of your color choices.** Bright colors get noticed, and wearing a lot of bright colors will really be noticed—and sometimes may get you labeled accordingly, as in the "red pants" illustration at the beginning of this chapter. You can wear color, of course; just don't let it overpower you. I'm tall, and if I wear a two-piece red suit, you can see me coming and going! That is not what I want to be remembered for. However, I can wear a red top with a black bottom.

8. **Do not wear T-shirts, shirts, or ties with inappropriate or offensive sayings or pictures.** You could insult someone. What you think is funny may not be universally accepted.

9. **Do not disregard your shoes.** People notice shoes. Your shoes should be clean, polished, and in good condition. This shows that you are paying attention to the details. Do not wear flip-flops or slippers. And women should stay away from ultra-high heels. A young student showed up for an evening class in five-inch heels. I couldn't believe she could wear them for work, so I asked her. She replied, "Oh, gosh, no. you can't wear these all day. They're for partying!"

10. **Do not dress inappropriately for business social events.** The company holiday party, conferences, the company picnic, and dinner at the boss's house are all business events, and your clothing choices matter. Whether you are going on an award cruise or attending a pool party with business associates, it's not the time to expose everything by wearing a bikini! This applies to both men and women.

Exercise

Go through your closet and consider its contents with this chapter in mind. Are there items you should stop wearing for work or work-related activities?

PRESCRIPTION FOR SUCCESS

Keep a dark jacket in your office. If you need to go somewhere for professional reasons and are dressed too casually, putting on the jacket will usually elevate your appearance.

94. Don't Take Your Neighbor's Bread, and Other Dining Suggestions

Is it okay to hit on the waitress during a business meal?

I have taught many dining etiquette seminars to business professionals and university students around the country and have learned not to be surprised by the topics people raise. The above question from a young man at a fraternity dinner brought a smile to my face. It is one of many questions that my participants have asked about how to handle themselves at business meals—though this one was a little more unusual than most.

The answer to the young man's question was a pleasant, "No . . . The dinner is a business activity." He smiled back and said, "I thought you would say that!"

Generally, the questions seminar participants ask are more involved, with many seeking an understanding of the correct placement of dishes and utensils. Here are some frequently asked questions and my answers:

Q. *How do I make sure I don't take my neighbor's bread?*

A. The good news is that when you are dining out, you don't set the table. You only have to read the place setting accurately to ensure that you use *your* bread-and-butter plate. An easy way to do this is to think of the "BMW" (Bread, Meal, Water). It will remind you that your bread-and-butter plate is on the left, and your water glass is on the right. And speaking of bread, do not cut it. Tear it in half, then break off a small piece at a time. When butter or oil is provided in a container shared by the table, place a portion on your bread plate for your individual use.

Q. *Why do I often see two forks at my place setting?*

A. Each course should have its own utensils. The largest fork is generally the entrée fork. The salad fork is smaller. And the general guideline is that you navigate your place setting by using the utensils from the outside in. In the United States, the salad fork is usually farthest from the plate, since you most often have salad before your main course. Depending on where in the world you are dining, the salad may be served after the main course, and then the fork placement would be switched.

Other utensils you may see in a place setting include a large entrée knife and a soup spoon, which is the largest spoon. Salad should be served in bite-sized pieces that may be eaten with the salad fork, but some restaurants also may include a smaller knife for your salad.

Q. *I sometimes see utensils above the plate. What are they?*

A. They are the dessert fork and spoon. Sometimes they may be placed on either side of the plate. At more casual restaurants, they may be brought in with the dessert.

Q. *When is it okay to take my napkin off the table and place it on my lap?*

A. If there is an official host for the meal, wait until she puts her napkin on her lap, and then do the same. This is the signal that the meal is officially beginning. If there is no host, place your napkin on your lap when you sit down. The waiter may also do this for you.

Q. *My colleague tells me he is eating correctly but he never puts his knife down. It looks strange. Is he correct?*

A. He may be. There are two ways to use your knife and fork for eating—the American style and the Continental style. In both styles, the utensils are held the same way for *cutting* your food. The shaft of the fork should be cradled in the palm of the hand,

and the fork maneuvered with the index finger and thumb. The knife is held the same way.

You *use* your utensils differently when eating American or Continental, and this difference is probably what you are noticing.

In the American style, you can cut up to three bite-size pieces of meat at a time, using both the knife and fork. You then place the knife at the top of the plate, switch the fork to your dominant hand, and use just the fork to pick up your food and bring it to your mouth.

In the Continental style, you also use both the knife and fork to cut your meat, one piece at a time. Do not put the knife down—you will use it to place food on the back of the fork for eating.

The colleague is probably using this latter style, which is appropriate in the United States—though not everyone is familiar with it.

Q. *In fancy restaurants I often get flustered when there are many courses being served. Any suggestions?*

A. First, familiarize yourself with the information above. Also, if you know that someone at your table has excellent table manners, discreetly follow that person's lead. If not, do what your hostess does.

Exercise

Play a dining game. Notice the different place settings whenever you dine out. Not all restaurants set the table the same way. Identify the utensils used, and also notice whether waiters bring the utensils for the courses you ordered. At a preset banquet, anticipate what you will be served by reading the place setting.

PRESCRIPTION FOR SUCCESS

Unless you are actually allergic to a specific food, don't refuse a course when you are dining internationally for business. In some cultures, turning down a dish may be interpreted as rude. If something looks unusual, eat a little and swallow quickly.

95. Be a Gracious Guest: 10 Ways to Avoid Dining Blunders

A new associate went out to dinner with her boss and a prospective client. At the table, she took her gum out of her mouth and stuck it to the underside of her dinner plate. She was no longer asked to attend dinner meetings.

A young graduate arrived slightly late for a luncheon group interview, then ordered the most expensive item on the menu. His meal arrived first, so he proceeded to eat before others got their meals. And then he didn't send a thank you note. He didn't get a job offer.

People can become quite nervous when they are dining for business. And for good reason. You don't want to lose a deal, a job offer, or your reputation based on your dining manners. Yet, so often I hear about blunders that professionals make at business meals, including the above vignettes.

Follow these suggestions to conduct yourself with poise and finesse when dining:

1. **Understand the purpose of a business meal.** Dining out with customers, clients, bosses, colleagues, or prospective employers is a business social activity. How you behave outside of the office will affect how others view you professionally. Remember, you are not there for the food—you are there for business.

2. **Don't be late.** Plan to arrive a little early. Greet your host, and shake hands correctly. Make sure you are dressed appropriately.

3. **Check the menu ahead of time if you have dietary restrictions.** Many restaurants list their menus on their websites. If you are

concerned about the ingredients in a particular dish, call the restaurant and ask how that food is prepared. You don't want to spend a lot of time at the table trying to decide what to order.

4. **Order wisely.** Don't order difficult-to-eat or messy meals. Avoid spaghetti, overstuffed sandwiches, and French onion soup. Order something you like that is also easy to eat. Don't exploit your host by ordering the most expensive thing on the menu. It is generally best to order something in the mid-price range, or a dish your host recommends.

5. **Practice good table manners.** Hold your knife and fork correctly. Understand place settings. Have good posture at the table. Do not talk with your mouth full, and do not use the napkin as a tissue. And no grooming at the table—excuse yourself and go to the restroom.

6. **Allow your host to get to know you.** Engage in conversation and find areas of common interest that can help establish rapport. Are you both into playing golf, traveling, or watching your kids play soccer? Also, know what is going on in your field and in the company. You want to be viewed as a knowledgeable professional.

7. **Be polite.** Don't yell at or be rude to the waiters. If you are rude to the server, why would I want to work with you? And don't criticize the restaurant or the food. If asked about a meal you don't particularly like, you can respond neutrally and say something like, "It's an interesting dish. I have never had it prepared this way."

8. **Don't drink too much.** Stay sober. When people get nervous, they sometimes drink to try to calm their nerves. Unfortunately, this can cloud their judgment, and they may end up saying or doing something they regret later.

9. **Understand the bill-paying process.** At a business meal, it is the host's responsibility to handle the check. (The host is the person who did the inviting.) As a guest, do not offer to split the bill or pay the tip.

10. **Thank your host, send a note of appreciation, and follow up with any promises you have made.** You appear gracious and reliable when you do.

QUESTION TO CONSIDER

Q. *I don't drink at all when entertaining for business. Better safe/sober than sorry. Is that a problem?*

A. It shouldn't be. You don't need to drink alcohol, but you do need to have a glass of something nonalcoholic in your hand or by your plate so that you are a part of the group and can participate in any toasts. You don't need to explain, either, though some colleagues can be very pushy in encouraging others to drink. I would then have a line ready to say, such as, "I am working later tonight" or "I'm the designated driver."

PRESCRIPTION FOR SUCCESS

Only send food back in extreme circumstances. You will embarrass your host and interrupt the flow of the meal. The other diners will be eating while you are waiting for your food. And when your substitute meal is served, they will be watching you eat.

96. Tips for Ordering Wine
at a Business Dinner

A colleague of mine sent me a news story about a man who ordered what he thought was a $37.50 bottle of wine, but unfortunately for him, the cost of the wine was $3,750. Big difference!

My seminar participant wasn't the only person amazed by this tale. The story was included in an article on MarketWatch, a website for business and finance news, about many people making wine-related blunders that turned out to be very costly. Here are some guidelines for ordering wine so you don't end up in a similar article:

1. **Do some research on wine.** You will make better choices, whether as host or guest, if you know something about the product. Books, websites, or classes at an adult education school or wine store can provide lots of information and help you gain confidence. Visits to wineries also can be helpful.

2. **If you are the host, you should choose the wine.** As mentioned above, knowing a little about wine will make your decision easier. You can ask the wine steward, or sommelier, to recommend some wines. It's part of the wine steward's job to help you make a wine selection appropriate for your food choices. Just make sure you are clear about the price!

   Participating in the wine-tasting process is also part of the host's responsibility. The wine steward will present the bottle's label for your review and then pour a small amount of wine into your glass. You should taste the wine and (usually) nod approval. Your guests' glasses are filled first, then yours. Send wine back only if it is spoiled.

Be cautious. It is easy to order additional, often unnecessary, bottles when you have had too much to drink.

3. **Check the wine list ahead of time.** Many restaurants post their wine lists on their websites. Pick a few bottles and research those. Though not all restaurants have prices on their website wine lists, your research should give you a general idea of the price range for a wine. Keep in mind, however, that restaurants mark up the price, so don't make any assumptions. And prices for the same wine may vary from vintage to vintage.

4. **Know your budget.** Have a general idea about what you want to spend before you go to the restaurant. There are many good, reasonably priced wines to be found. Look for wine that you have enjoyed before. And remember that the most expensive bottle on the list is not always the best. If you are celebrating a big occasion, or your guest loves a certain wine, you may choose to increase your budget. You can give the wine steward your price range by pointing at a price—not a wine—and saying something like, "I was looking for something like this."

5. **Be wary of deferring to your guest.** He or she may order a bottle with a price that exceeds your budget.

QUESTION TO CONSIDER

Q. Is it ever inappropriate to order wine with a meal?

A. Generally, if you are dining in a nice restaurant, it is appropriate to order wine with dinner. If you know your guests don't drink, you may not want to do so. Mostly, wine is not ordered at lunch meetings because it is accepted that people have to return to work.

Exercise

Keep a wine diary. Record what you have tasted and your opinions about the wine. Over time you will gain a lot of knowledge. You can buy special journals that make this very easy to do.

PRESCRIPTION FOR SUCCESS

The more you know about wine, the more you can be adventurous with your wine pairings. Although conventional wisdom says that white wine goes with fish or poultry and red wine with red meat, that is a very general guideline.

97. In a Restaurant, to Introduce or Not? Tips for a Tricky Etiquette Situation

During a meal with some colleagues, a man stopped at my table to greet me. I didn't introduce him to the other people at the table. His body posture (he was following someone and had his body turned semi-away from the table) seemed to convey he was moving on. Should I have made introductions? What do you do when people stop by your table when you are dining with others?

A colleague emailed me for some help about the above situation that easily can become awkward when people are dining out for business.

It's natural for people who see others they know to want to greet them. It can feel rude if they don't. Generally, all that is needed in a restaurant is a brief acknowledgment, a "Hello," possibly followed by a quick comment or two.

If a polite greeter becomes an "interrupter" by staying at the table beyond a brief exchange, the person's presence can affect the flow of the meal. Not only does the interruption disrupt the conversation at the table, potentially causing discomfort for those not included in the new conversation, but it also allows the diners' food to grow cold.

If introductions are attempted, polite diners attempting to rise to acknowledge the interrupter can easily knock over glasses or dishes on the table. Clearly, this is a situation to be avoided if possible—unless, of course, the "interrupter" is your CEO, in which case by all means invite him or her to join you.

Here are a few general guidelines to help you to manage a potential interrupter. They work equally well for business or social occasions:

1. You usually don't need to make an introduction if the interruption is very brief. In my colleague's situation, it was clear that the man was moving on.

2. If your conversation with an interrupter goes beyond a brief comment or two, you need to make introductions. You should mention the name of the other person at your table first, and say something like, "Ryan, this is Melanie Jones. We worked together at ABC Company. Melanie, this is Ryan Johnson, my new boss."

3. Ideally, people realize that they are interrupting others and keep their conversation to a minimum. If you get the sense that the person wants to talk, you can say something like, "It has been really nice seeing you. Let's catch up next week."

PRESCRIPTION FOR SUCCESS

When making introductions, mention the name of your host or the higher-ranking person first—regardless of gender. Decisions on how men and women interact in the business world are no longer based on gender, but much more on rank or host/visitor status.

98. Your Mother Was Right: The Importance of Expressing Thanks

When I forget my E-Z pass, I say "thank you" to the ticket machines on the New Jersey Turnpike!

I will admit it: Since I teach etiquette, I say "thank you" a lot. Saying it to machines may be overkill, but in the business world, and elsewhere, it is important to express thanks, whether it's in words or writing.

If someone helps you, wishes you well, or gives you a compliment, it's polite to say "thank you." And it is rude if you don't. You are acknowledging the person's actions or comments. You can, of course, add more. Good lines include:

Thank you. Your help made all the difference in making the deadline.

Thanks. Your feedback means a lot to me.

Thank you. Let me know when I can return the favor.

If you are not able to speak to the person, or you want to emphasize your appreciation, you can write a note. And etiquette requires that you write a thank you note if you receive a gift, visit the home of a boss or colleague, are a guest at a meal, or interview for a job.

An email thank you is quick and informal. A handwritten note is more personal, is slower to arrive, and often stands out in our high-tech world.

Effective notes express the reason the person is writing and mention what the gift, service, item, or kindness meant to him or her. Here are some examples:

Thank you for a lovely lunch today. Not only was the food enjoyable, but you helped me to understand very clearly what would be required of me if a position opens up in your department. I really appreciate your thinking of me for this potential role.

I have been meaning to write to you regarding your Effective Business Writing class. I just wanted to let you know what a great job you did in keeping the class interested and getting your lessons across. I must say I was not expecting to be even the slightest bit interested in this class, and was shocked at how much I learned and at how satisfied I was with the course. That being said, I wanted to say thank you for a great class, and I look forward to your future classes.

Keep these points in mind when expressing thanks:

1. **Send or email thank you notes.** Your appreciation needs to be timely.

2. **Make sure your note is error-free.** Make sure there are no typos. Your credibility will be affected if your note includes misspelled words or poor grammar.

3. **Be mindful that there can be negative consequences if you don't express thanks.** One man said that he went out of his way to help a colleague finish a report. She never thanked him—in person or in writing. He noticed her lack of courtesy, and it affected how he viewed her professionally.

QUESTION TO CONSIDER

Q. *If you think someone is giving you an insincere compliment, should you say thank you?*

A. Absolutely. Whether sincere or insincere, acknowledge the person's nice words. If the compliment is truly sarcastic, still say thank you. You are responding to what was said—and if it wasn't meant kindly, your thanks is likely to frustrate the other person!

Exercise

Save the thank you notes you receive. There are two reasons for this: If you like the wording of a note, it can provide a general template for when you write your notes. The second reason is that you can reread the notes when you are feeling low—it's sure to give you a morale boost.

PRESCRIPTION FOR SUCCESS

Saying please is important, too. What would you rather hear, "Get this to me by 3 p.m." or "Please get this to me by 3 p.m."? Every person I ever asked preferred hearing the request with the "please." But please, please, please, don't beg. You only need to say please once!

99. Etiquette for Hallways, Sidewalks, and Other Walkways

While walking to work, I saw a woman with her friend heading toward me. As we passed, the woman who was dominating most of the sidewalk failed to move over and as a result jammed into my shoulder. Ouch!

This happened to me, but I have heard similar stories from employees about navigating the hallways at work.

Sharing public space, whether it's on sidewalks or in hallways, is a common cause of conflict and an ongoing concern for pedestrians and office workers alike.

The *New York Times* wrote about this problem some years ago, and the *Village Voice* once ran a tongue-in-cheek article about the (fake) New York Department of Pedestrian Etiquette, which would require all pedestrians to receive etiquette training for navigating the city's walkways.

I don't think most people who crowd colleagues or fellow pedestrians are deliberately trying to be rude—they're often unaware of their behavior and how it affects others. Yet if we want things to change, the change starts with us. You don't need official training to learn to negotiate common spaces politely. You simply need to follow these guidelines:

1. **Make room for others.** If you are walking with other people and taking up most or all of the hallway or sidewalk, it is your responsibility to make room for any other person coming toward you. In doing so, don't wait until the last moment. Move over before you bump into someone.

2. **Pay attention to your surroundings.** When you stop to chat with people, don't block the hallway or sidewalk. You should move to

one side so others can pass. People shouldn't have to walk around you or push past you.

3. **Don't walk and text on the phone.** One professor said that students on their phones constantly bump into her in her school's narrow hallways. She noted that when texting, her students become oblivious of others. And it's not just students: One woman in Florida walked into the path of a freight train while texting! Amazingly, she survived.

4. **Don't cut too closely when passing someone.** Doing so can be startling to the person you are cutting in front of—and the heels of your shoes may be stepped on.

5. **Acknowledge other people.** If you make eye contact with someone, say "hello" or "good morning," smile, or nod to the person. When you do so, you are letting him or her into your space, and you are less likely to bump into that person. Remember, you don't need to know someone to say hello. One woman told me that when she smiles at people she doesn't know who have mean looks on their faces, most often they smile back and don't look so mean anymore.

6. **Don't stop suddenly.** People will bump into you.

PRESCRIPTION FOR SUCCESS

Sharing the space extends to roadways, too — but it's the pedestrian who must be extra vigilant. When traveling in other countries, remember to look both ways before you cross the street. Depending where you are in the world, cars could be coming in the opposite direction from the one you are familiar with. People have gotten hit because they were not paying attention.

Conclusion

I am writing on article on careers. What are the most important things to mention?

I can't implement everything you suggest all at once. What are the important things to remember right now?

If I could only tell my students 10 things, what would they be?

Many people, including reporters, colleagues, businesspeople, professors, and students, have asked versions of the questions above. There is a lot to learn in this book, so it only seems fitting to end the book with a list of our top 10 pieces of advice for business professionals.

1. **Have "fire in your belly."** Have a powerful sense of determination—of working hard to succeed. Some people seem to be born with this attribute; others have to create it. To ignite that blaze, go above and beyond. Do more than what is expected of you. Show initiative and do good work.

2. **Learn to command the room.** Walk into a room like you belong there. Stand tall. Don't fidget. Speak loudly enough to be heard. Dress appropriately. Shake hands correctly. Offer your opinion. If you don't speak up in meetings, people won't know what you know.

3. **Build your career.** Develop your network, both online and off. Have mentors and role models. Join professional associations. Apply for awards. Have a complete LinkedIn profile. Develop an area of expertise.

4. **Separate from your phone at times.** Keep your phone off the table when meeting with someone. Having your phone visible tells the other person, "I am *so* ready to drop you and connect with someone else." Don't walk and text, either.

5. **Be friendly and helpful.** Greet people you know and don't know. Smile. Say "please" and "thank you." Send thank you notes. Acknowledge others' successes. Help people when you can. Make connections for others, both online and in person.

6. **Don't allow social media to hurt your career.** Post smartly. If you use Facebook, Instagram, Pinterest, and so on for your personal activities, your colleagues or potential employers may see your posts to these sites and judge you accordingly. If you appear to drink too much, curse a lot, or post nasty comments, people may question whether they want to work with you or hire you.

7. **Make presentations.** The more presentations you make, the more comfortable you will become. And they don't have to be work presentations—any presentation, as a volunteer or to a community organization, will be good practice in speaking in front of others.

8. **Email professionally.** Include a salutation and closing. Use "reply all" only when it is necessary for everyone on the list to see the email. Proofread carefully—*before* you press send. Make sure your writings are error-free. Remember AIL—address in last. Stop the email trail when the sender of the email no longer needs to be acknowledged or thanked.

9. **Spend time on your job search.** Have an up-to-date, error-free résumé. Google yourself to see what prospective employers will see. Let your network know you are looking. Practice interviewing.

10. **Attend business social events.** How you behave outside of the office will affect how others view you professionally. Mingle. You never know whom you may meet. Don't order messy meals, and do stay sober. Remember, you are not there for the food—you are there for business.

Important as they are, these 10 suggestions are only the beginning. This book highlights the knowledge we have gained from years of interacting with colleagues and workers at all levels. It is a privilege to share this information with you. We believe it will help you to maximize your potential and make the most of your career. We encourage you to keep this reference handy, and to dip into it often for advice to help you grow as a professional.

Good luck on that journey.

To connect with Barbara Pachter via social media:

www.pachter.com

www.facebook.com/pachtertraining

www.twitter.com/barbarapachter

www.linkedin.com/in/barbarapachter

www.pachter.com/blog

Pachter & Associates, PO Box 3680, Cherry Hill, NJ 08034, 856.751.6141

Feel free to send me your suggestions and experiences at bpachter@pachter.com.

Index

About the Authors

Barbara Pachter
Speaker, Author, and Coach

Barbara Pachter is an internationally-renowned business etiquette and communications speaker and coach. She has delivered more than 2,500 seminars throughout the world including the first-ever seminar for businesswomen in Kuwait. Pachter is also adjunct faculty in the School of Business at Rutgers University and Coadjutant Lecturer in the Ernest Mario School of Pharmacy.

Her client list boasts many of today's most notable organizations, including Bayer HealthCare, Campbell Soup, Children's Hospital of Philadelphia, Chrysler, Cisco Systems, Cleveland Clinic, Con Edison, Ecolab, Microsoft, Novartis, Pfizer, Princeton University, and Wawa.

Pachter is the author of 10 books, including *The Essentials of Business Etiquette: How to Greet, Eat, and Tweet Your Way to Success* and *The Power of Positive Confrontation*. Her books have been translated into 11 languages.

She is quoted regularly in newspapers and magazines, including the *Wall Street Journal*, the *New York Times*, and *TIME Magazine*, and she has appeared on ABC's *20/20*, *The TODAY Show*, and *The Early Show*. Her discussion on business etiquette appeared in the *Harvard Business Review*. She is a contributor to *Business Insider*.

Pachter's areas of expertise include presentation skills, business etiquette, assertive communication, business writing, positive confrontation, business dress, career development, and women in the workplace. She holds undergraduate and graduate degrees from the University of Michigan and completed postgraduate studies in the Middle East and at Temple University. Pachter is a former ESL teacher.

She can be contacted at Pachter & Associates, PO Box 3680, Cherry Hill, NJ 08034, USA, 856-751-6141, bpachter@pachter.com, www.pachter.com.

Denise Cowie
Writer and Editor

Denise Cowie is a transplanted Australian who has lived most of her adult life as a journalist in the United States. She has worked on three continents, including many years at the *Philadelphia Inquirer*, where her assignments included a range of editing roles as well as several years as a feature writer and columnist. After leaving daily journalism, she added to her resume by managing a website for a nonprofit consortium of public gardens, as well as writing or editing for magazines, books, and websites.

She has served on the boards of several nonprofit organizations. She is a Fellow of the Garden Writers Association of North America, and she also has been a judge for that organization's national media awards.

Also by Barbara Pachter and Denise Cowie

The Definitive Guide to Professional Behavior

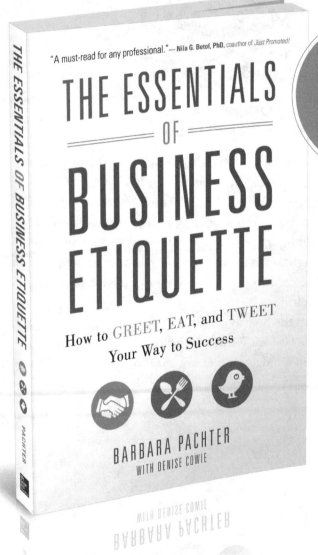

"A must-read for any professional." —Nila G. Betof, PhD, coauthor of *Just Promoted!*

THE ESSENTIALS
OF
BUSINESS
ETIQUETTE

How to GREET, EAT, and TWEET
Your Way to Success

BARBARA PACHTER
WITH DENISE COWIE

Whether you're eating lunch with a client, Skyping with your boss, or meeting a business partner for the first time — it's all about how you present yourself. Here are 101 critical business behavior tips, all delivered in a quick, no-nonsense format.

Learn More, Do More.
mhprofessional.com

Mc
Graw
Hill
Education